T0373793

FIREPIT BARBECUE

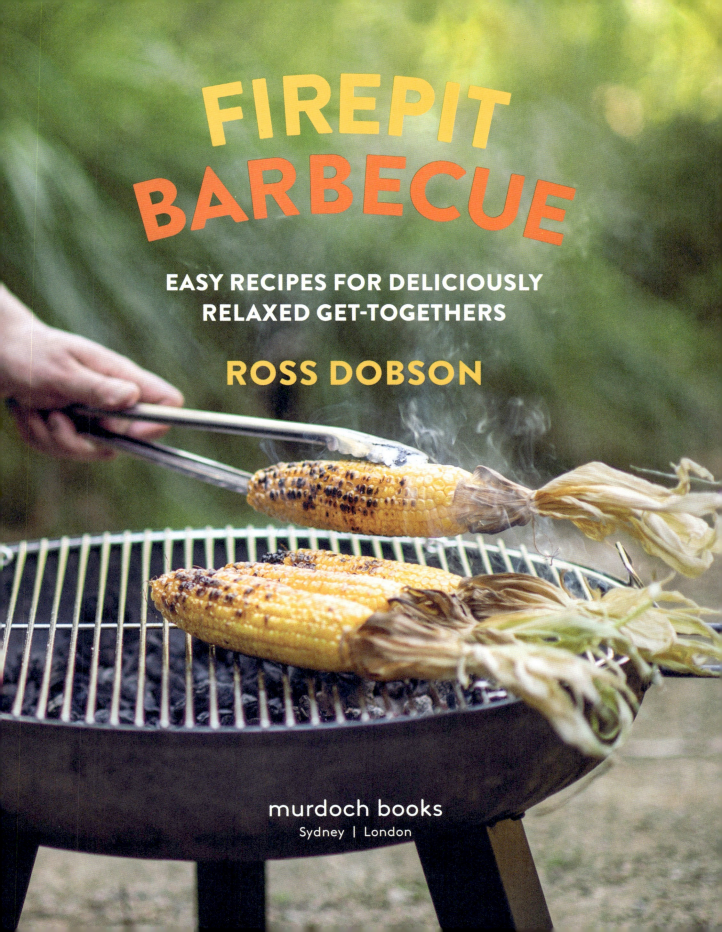

FIREPIT BARBECUE

EASY RECIPES FOR DELICIOUSLY RELAXED GET-TOGETHERS

ROSS DOBSON

murdoch books

Sydney | London

CONTENTS

Firepit cooking 7

Chicken and other poultry 12

Beef, pork and lamb 64

Seafood 110

Vegies 144

Bits and bobs 190

Index 202

FIREPIT COOKING

What is a firepit?

In the most basic sense, a firepit is just that: a pit of fire. What started as a simple hole in the ground, in which burning wood supplied heat for warmth and cooking, has become over the centuries more practical and safe through design. What many of us think of as a firepit is simply a vessel that burns wood, over which a suspended grill or hotplate can be fitted to cook food.

I've seen the most basic of firepits — nothing more than a recycled metal drum with holes punched in the side to supply air flow and enable the wood to burn (remember: a fire needs oxygen). A grill, such as an old cooking grill from an oven, is placed on top of the metal drum. Once the smoke and flames have subsided, it is ready to cook food over the heat emitted from the hot charcoal.

It is the heat from the charcoal that is required for cooking. You will notice that when wood is burning, it's almost as if it's alive: it hisses, spits and groans. These noises are made by the burning of the minerals and water in the wood, and the side effect of this is smoke. Smoke, and soot, is released while the volatiles in the wood are still burning away. And smoke is something you don't want when you're cooking on an open firepit. Cooking on a smoky fire gives an unpleasant diesel-like taste to the food. When the noise and smoke subsides, you are left with charcoal, which burns at a higher temperature than wood and should glow and pulse with heat. It will have few visible flames, releasing only pure heat. It takes time to achieve this, and patience is required.

Timber for your firepit

You might think wood is wood — but there are many different types of trees. Soft timber from trees such as cypress, pine and fir burns too quickly and is no good for the firepit. These woods might be less expensive, but they won't go the distance. Do not burn treated timber from trees, and from other large plants that are toxic. Many of us may know that oleander, for example, is toxic, and shouldn't be burnt anywhere near people. The same goes for any treated or painted timber.

In Australia and New Zealand the best timber to burn is hardwood gum or eucalyptus. In Australia timber varies slightly from state to state. Generally speaking, the timbers that burn the longest are jarrah, iron bark, box and river red gum.

The same applies when choosing timber for burning in North America, the United Kingdom and Europe. Timber with the least pitch (resin) or sap is the best choice for burning on the firepit. In North America this is timber from maple, ash, birch and oak. The most widely available timbers for burning in the United Kingdom and Europe are similar to North America, but also include fruit trees with hard timber, such as cherry and apple.

The best wood for burning will feel dense, it should be grey in colour (definitely not green), hollow sounding when two logs are tapped together, and free of fibrous bark, or at least indications that bark can be broken away easily. What you are looking for is wood that is as dry as possible. Green wood, or wood with some bark attached, indicates there is moisture in the wood, which will produce more smoke and requires more energy to burn off the water and minerals. Worse still, it might not even burn at all. Always go for grey, dry and dense.

Preparing the firepit for cooking

Many modern firepits will come with an attachable grill, which is perfect for cooking. Remove the grill while you fire up the coals. Take two medium-sized pieces of firewood and place them in the centre of the firepit, parallel to each other and about 20 cm (8 inches) apart. Take two more similar-sized pieces of wood and place these on top, in the opposite direction, parallel and 20 cm (8 inches) apart. There will be a gap in the centre — this is where you ignite the fire.

Crumple up some newspaper into loose balls and put these between the timber (egg cartons work a treat, too). Now arrange some kindling around the paper to look like a tee pee. Light the newspaper in several places, allowing it to catch and burn — it won't take long before the kindling catches fire, but the large pieces of timber will need some more time. You can use a piece of cardboard or a baking tray to fan air into the fire and encourage it to burn.

Timber needs air and space to burn so don't overcrowd it. Give it time and space to turn into coals. It is not wood per se that you need to cook with; it's what the wood becomes.

When is the firepit ready?

Over a period of about 2 hours, the timber becomes black and ultimately turns into charcoal. It will break up into small pieces and is supercharged with energy and glows with intense heat. Coals about the size of a golf ball, and no larger than a tennis ball, are what you are looking for to cook with. And, unlike wood, which needs space to burn, these hot coals work best when pushed together to generate and maintain optimum heat for cooking.

The easiest way to test if your firepit is ready for cooking is to trust your own senses. Firstly, use your eyes: you want to see small pieces of red-hot coals with a minimal amount of smoke. Secondly, use your sense of touch. Put the palm of your hand about 5–10 cm (2–4 inches) over the centre of the firepit. You should only be able to hold your hand there for some 2–3 seconds. Replace the grill over the firepit and give it around 10 minutes to heat up.

What tools do you need?

You can treat the firepit like any open fireplace you have inside the house. That is, you might have a fireplace kit which can include a hand shovel, ember movers, bellows. These will all be useful – but not necessary. I personally find something that is long and made of metal to poke the fire is essential, plus a couple of pairs of long metal cooking tongs. A dustpan and brush is always good to have on hand for cleaning up, once the firepit is completely cool. If your firepit is small enough, you might be able to tip the burnt-out coals and ash directly into your organic refuse bin or onto a compost heap. My local council provides large bins for organic matter and these accept ash.

What to cook on a firepit

You can cook almost everything that you can cook on a conventional barbecue. But, do remember that the firepit does not have a lid that can close and trap in heat, acting like an oven of sorts. Keep in mind that smaller cuts of meat cook best on a firepit. Chicken fillet is ideal; darker thigh meat, with lines of fat, is ideal. You can, of course, use chicken breast fillet, but I personally find this too dry and not as flavoursome as thigh. Cute little trimmed lamb cutlets are perfect. The bone is all ready to use as a utensil to hold the chop and wolf down the tender meat. Pork and beef cutlets are good, too, as are most fillets of red meat: lamb, beef and pork.

While larger bits of meat can be cooked on the firepit, they do require more attention and patience. To ensure large dense cuts of meat are cooked through, a good tip is to wrap the seared meat in foil and move to the edge of the firepit. Here the heat is less intense and the meat can cook through without burning.

Many vegetables are perfect for cooking on the firepit. Whole or thickly sliced eggplant (aubergine) and capsicum (pepper) are ideal; so too are root vegetables like sweet potato and potato, wrapped in foil and ready to be smothered in butter, sour cream, yoghurt or labneh. Sweetcorn, too, cooks to perfection on the firepit. Patiently turn the corn over the heat until the kernels burst with a golden flavour that's hard to beat.

With seafood, large prawns and lobsters fair well, especially when left in their shell, which acts as a natural protective armour. Delicate white fish fillets are best wrapped in a foil parcel, and need very little cooking time. For drama, the firepit is the way to go for cooking your favourite whole fish. Again, whole fish is best wrapped in some sort of parcel made of baking paper with an outside layer of foil. (The paper-thin skin of many fish will stick to cooking foil and it can prove very tricky to peel off once the fish is cooked; hence the baking paper on the inside.) These sturdy parcels also make it easier to transfer the fish from the firepit to a serving platter.

Ross Dobson

HONEY HOISIN CHICKEN.........................14

BUCCANEER CHICKEN SKEWERS...........17

CHILLI CHICKEN BLT................................18

FRAGRANT CHICKEN PARCELS..............21

TANDOORI CHICKEN
WITH CHEAT'S GARLIC NAAN..................22

LEMONGRASS AND
LIME LEAF CHICKEN.................................25

CHIMICHURRI CHOOK.............................26

BLACKENED BIRD......................................29

QUAIL WITH PEANUT AND
THAI HERB PESTO......................................30

LEBANESE CHICKEN
WITH TOUM..31

FESTIVE TURKEY...32

SPICED QUAIL WITH VIETNAMESE
LIME AND PEPPER DIPPING SAUCE.......35

TERIYAKI AND BEER CHICKEN...............36

LEMON CHICKEN, FETA
AND HERB ROLLS..39

PIRI PIRI SPATCHCOCK.............................40

FIREPIT CHICKEN
WITH GREEN OLIVE SALSA VERDE........43

CHILLI YOGHURT CHICKEN....................44

HARISSA CHICKEN......................................45

GREEN CURRY CHICKEN..........................46

THAI BARBECUED CHICKEN....................49

CHICKEN WITH
JALAPENO BUTTER.....................................50

CHINATOWN DUCK SHANKS...................53

CHICKEN SHAWARMA...............................54

KERALAN CHICKEN....................................57

COCONUT TENDERLOINS........................58

SWEET CHILLI AND
GINGER CHICKEN.......................................59

FIERY CHICKEN CHOPS............................60

CREOLE CHICKEN.......................................63

CHICKEN AND OTHER POULTRY

HONEY HOISIN CHICKEN

This recipe involves a simple butchering trick to ensure the chicken thigh is the same thickness all over so that it cooks evenly on the fire. The thinner the piece of chicken, the larger the surface area ... which means more flavour from the marinade.

SERVES 4

8 skinless boneless chicken thighs

3 tablespoons hoisin sauce

3 tablespoons light soy sauce

2 teaspoons dark soy sauce

3 tablespoons runny honey

3 tablespoons Chinese black vinegar

4 garlic cloves, roughly chopped

1 tablespoon finely grated ginger

4 large dried chillies

4 large fresh chillies

1 handful coriander (cilantro) sprigs

To prepare the chicken thighs, put them on a chopping board, smooth side down (the smooth side is where the skin once was). You should be able to easily see the thicker part of the thigh. Use a small sharp knife to butterfly this part of the thigh, so the thigh is then an even thickness all over.

Combine the hoisin, soy sauces, honey, vinegar, garlic and ginger in a bowl. Break the dried chillies into small pieces and add to the bowl. Season with salt and freshly ground black pepper. Add the chicken to the bowl and toss together with your hands. Cover and refrigerate for 3–6 hours. Remove from the fridge 30 minutes before cooking.

Your firepit is ready to cook on after about 2 hours of burning, when the timber is charcoal black, has transformed into red hot coals about the size of golf balls, and the smoke has all but subsided. To test for heat, you should not be able to hold the palm of your hand 5–10 cm (2–4 inches) above the grill for more than 2–3 seconds. Replace the grill over the firepit and give it around 10 minutes to heat up. (See page 9.)

Lay the chicken thighs on a hot part of the grill. Cook for 8 minutes. Turn and cook for a further 5 minutes. Transfer to a plate and cover with foil for 5 minutes. Meanwhile, put the whole chillies on the grill and cook for 8–10 minutes, turning every couple of minutes until they soften.

Arrange the grilled chillies around the chicken and scatter with coriander.

BUCCANEER CHICKEN SKEWERS

To me, Caribbean food means hot cayenne pepper and tropical lime, which brings to mind buccaneers. Thread the chicken onto long metal skewers — Brazilian churrasco skewers are ideal, and, at a stretch, they do resemble pirate swords. Alternatively, use wooden skewers soaked in water for 1 hour before cooking.

SERVES 4

6 skinless boneless chicken thighs

2 spring onions (scallions), chopped

1 handful flat-leaf (Italian) parsley

2 garlic cloves, chopped

¼ teaspoon cayenne pepper

2 tablespoons lime juice

2 tablespoons olive oil

LIME CHILLI SAUCE

3 tablespoons lime juice

2 tablespoons olive oil

3 tablespoons finely chopped flat-leaf (Italian) parsley

2 teaspoons finely chopped rosemary

1 large red chilli, finely chopped

4 spring onions (scallions), thinly sliced

Cut each chicken thigh into 4 equal pieces and put in a non-metallic bowl. In a food processor, mix the spring onions, parsley, garlic, cayenne pepper, lime juice and olive oil to a paste. Rub all over the chicken. Cover and refrigerate for at least 6 hours.

To make the lime chilli sauce, combine all the ingredients in a bowl with 125 ml (4 fl oz) boiling water. Stir well.

Thread the chicken onto 2 long metal churrasco skewers, or soaked bamboo skewers.

Your firepit is ready to cook on after about 2 hours of burning, when the timber is charcoal black, has transformed into red hot coals about the size of golf balls, and the smoke has all but subsided. To test for heat, you should not be able to hold the palm of your hand 5–10 cm (2–4 inches) above the grill for more than 2–3 seconds. Replace the grill over the firepit and give it around 10 minutes to heat up. (See page 9.)

Lay the skewers on the grill and cook for 12–15 minutes, turning every couple of minutes, until the chicken is golden and cooked through. Leave on the skewers for a touch of drama, or slide onto a serving plate and serve with the sauce.

CHILLI CHICKEN BLT

Firepit chicken is a great new spin on the old bacon, lettuce and tomato BLT — perfect for a winter morning brunch or camping supper. You can make the chilli marinade the day before and leave the chicken in it overnight to gather flavour.

SERVES 4

2 skinless boneless chicken breasts

2 large red chillies, seeded and chopped

2 garlic cloves, chopped

1 handful flat-leaf (Italian) parsley leaves, roughly chopped

3 tablespoons olive oil

4 rashers streaky bacon

4 soft bread rolls

Mayonnaise, to serve

2 large handfuls baby rocket (arugula)

2 tomatoes, thinly sliced

Lay the chicken on a clean chopping board. Gently press the palm of your hand on the chicken and use a sharp knife to slice it horizontally into 2 thinner pieces. Put into a bowl.

Combine the chillies, garlic and parsley in a small food processor. Add the olive oil and whiz until the mixture is finely chopped and flecked through the oil. Tip into the bowl with the chicken and toss together with your hands. Cover and refrigerate for at least 6 hours.

Just before cooking, wrap each chicken breast in a rasher of bacon.

Your firepit is ready to cook on after about 2 hours of burning, when the timber is charcoal black, has transformed into red hot coals about the size of golf balls, and the smoke has all but subsided. To test for heat, you should not be able to hold the palm of your hand 5—10 cm (2—4 inches) above the grill for more than 2—3 seconds. Replace the grill over the firepit and give it around 10 minutes to heat up. (See page 9.)

Lay the chicken on the grill and cook for 8 minutes. Turn and cook for a further 4—5 minutes, until the chicken is cooked through and the bacon done.

Serve the chicken on rolls spread with mayonnaise and topped with rocket and tomato.

FRAGRANT CHICKEN PARCELS

This recipe offers some classic Chinese flavours: sweet and salty with intense aromatics. The chicken tenderloins are wrapped and steamed on the hotplate over the firepit. I love cooking with tenderloins: they often don't need any cutting or chopping and I use them all the time in curries. I don't even brown them first — just throw then into the hot curry and leave them to poach.

SERVES 4

12 chicken tenderloins

8 garlic cloves, peeled but left whole

3 tablespoons light soy sauce

50 g (1¾ oz) unsalted butter, melted

2 tablespoons runny honey

4 star anise

2 cinnamon sticks, broken in half

1 handful coriander (cilantro) sprigs

Put all the ingredients in a bowl, tossing to combine. Set aside at room temperature for 30 minutes, or cover and refrigerate for up to 6 hours. Remove from the fridge 30 minutes before you begin cooking.

Tear off 4 large sheets of foil and lay on a work surface. Tear off 4 large sheets of baking paper and lay on top of the foil.

Put 3 tenderloins in the centre of each sheet of baking paper. Use the foil to form a cup shape around the chicken. Spoon equal amounts of marinade over each portion of chicken. Twist the foil to secure and enclose to make a parcel.

Your firepit is ready to cook on after about 2 hours of burning, when the timber is charcoal black, has transformed into red hot coals about the size of golf balls, and the smoke has all but subsided. To test for heat, you should not be able to hold the palm of your hand 5–10 cm (2–4 inches) above the grill for more than 2–3 seconds. Replace the grill over the firepit and give it around 10 minutes to heat up. (See page 9.)

Sit the chicken parcels on the hotplate section and cook for 20 minutes. Remove and leave wrapped for 5 minutes before serving. Garnish with fresh coriander leaves. This is excellent with grilled corn.

TANDOORI CHICKEN WITH CHEAT'S GARLIC NAAN

A firepit comes as close as you can get at home to achieving the smoky goodness of a real tandoor oven. For this recipe you need a grill and a hotplate section over your fire. The longer the marinating time here, the better the flavour. So, if you do have the chance, get this happening the day before.

SERVES 8

8 chicken marylands

1 teaspoon saffron threads

½ cup (125 ml) lemon juice

3 teaspoons sea salt

2 onions, chopped

1 cup (260 g) plain yoghurt

2 tablespoons ghee

2 garlic cloves, chopped

1 tablespoon finely grated ginger

2 teaspoons ground cumin

1 teaspoon ground coriander

½ teaspoon ground turmeric

½ teaspoon chilli powder

Lemon wedges, to serve

CHEAT'S GARLIC NAAN

½ cup (125 g) unsalted butter

1 tablespoon finely chopped garlic

8 naan breads

Cut several diagonal slashes in the skin side of each maryland and put onto a baking tray.

Soak the saffron threads in 2 tablespoons of hot water for 10 minutes.

Combine the lemon juice, sea salt and saffron mixture in a small bowl and rub into the skin side of the chicken. Put the chicken in the fridge and leave for 1 hour.

Put the onions, yoghurt, ghee, garlic, ginger, cumin, coriander, turmeric and chilli powder in a food processor and blend to a paste. Rub this all over the chicken. Leave uncovered and return the chicken to the fridge for 6 hours or overnight. Remove 30 minutes before cooking.

Your firepit is ready to cook on after about 2 hours of burning, when the timber is charcoal black, has transformed into red hot coals about the size of golf balls, and the smoke has all but subsided. To test for heat, you should not be able to hold the palm of your hand 5–10 cm (2–4 inches) above the grill for more than 2–3 seconds. Replace the grill over the firepit and give it around 10 minutes to heat up. (See page 9.)

Put the chicken, skin side down, on the grill. Cook for 10 minutes. Move around on the grill if need be to avoid burning. Turn over and cook for a further 10 minutes. Turn over and move to the edge of the grill, where the heat is less intense. Cook for 5 minutes, then turn and cook for a further 5 minutes, until cooked through. Serve with lemon wedges and garlic naan on the side.

CHEAT'S GARLIC NAAN

Combine the butter and garlic in a small saucepan on the grill of your firepit. Leave until the butter starts to bubble.

Brush one side of each naan with garlic butter and lay on the hotplate, butter side down. Use tongs to have a peek at the bread and cook until it is golden or charred to your liking. Turn over and cook the unbuttered side until golden.

LEMONGRASS AND LIME LEAF CHICKEN

If you live somewhere temperate, it is easy to grow lemongrass and it is much better when picked and used fresh. The top green part of lemongrass is more fibrous and less flavoursome, so use the soft white part, close to the bottom. If you live near an Asian food store, ask if they have frozen lemongrass — it is an excellent product.

SERVES 4

6 skinless boneless chicken thighs

2 lemongrass stalks, white part only, finely sliced

4 small makrut lime leaves, very finely shredded

3 garlic cloves, chopped

1 tablespoon grated ginger

2 spring onions (scallions), chopped

1 tablespoon olive oil

1 tablespoon fish sauce

8 squares of banana leaf, each 30 cm (12 inches) square

Lime wedges, to serve

Cut each chicken thigh into 4 equal pieces. Put into a bowl.

Put the lemongrass, makrut leaves, garlic, ginger and spring onions in a food processor and whiz into a fibrous and chunky paste. Add the oil and fish sauce and mix to combine. Pour over the chicken and toss together.

Cover and refrigerate for at least 6 hours, turning often. Remove from the fridge 20 minutes before cooking.

To soften the banana leaves so they fold easily, put them in a clean sink or bowl and cover them with boiling water. When cool enough to handle, shake dry. Lay a banana leaf square on a work surface, then another over the top, at diagonals, to make a star shape. Put 6 pieces of chicken in the centre of each leaf star. Pour over any marinade that is left. Bring the corners of the banana leaf stars together and seal with toothpicks to make parcels.

Your firepit is ready to cook on after about 2 hours of burning, when the timber is charcoal black, has transformed into red hot coals about the size of golf balls, and the smoke has all but subsided. To test for heat, you should not be able to hold the palm of your hand 5—10 cm (2—4 inches) above the grill for more than 2—3 seconds. Replace the grill over the firepit and give it around 10 minutes to heat up. (See page 9.)

Sit the parcels on your grill and cook for 15—20 minutes, until the chicken is cooked through. Transfer to a serving platter and leave for 5 minutes. Serve with lime wedges.

CHIMICHURRI CHOOK

Chimichurri is the stuff of folklore and urban myth — you will find this South American staple smothered on grilled chorizo and served in crusty bread rolls in Argentina. It is great with turkey, chicken, fish and any grilled meats. One reference claims that, for the sauce to be authentic, the marinated meat should taste as if it has been dragged through the garden! Another tale goes that it was named after an Irishman by the name of Jimmy Curry. (Say it quickly enough, after a few drinks on a warm day, and it might make sense.) I am using chimichurri as a marinade here but you can serve it as a condiment with pretty much anything. It's also good dolloped on top of a baked potato with sour cream.

SERVES 4

4 boneless chicken breasts, skin on

Lemon wedges, to serve

CHIMICHURRI

2 garlic cloves, chopped

½ teaspoon sea salt

1 small handful flat-leaf (Italian) parsley, chopped

1 tablespoon chopped oregano leaves

1 small handful coriander (cilantro), chopped

¼ teaspoon cayenne pepper

¼ teaspoon sweet paprika

3 tablespoons olive oil

3 tablespoons red wine vinegar

To make the chimichurri, put the garlic, salt, herbs, spices and olive oil in a food processor and process to a chunky paste. With the motor running, add the red wine vinegar. Transfer to a bowl, cover and refrigerate until ready to serve (can be kept for up to 2 days, but the fresh flavours are best on the day of making).

Cut each chicken breast into 4–6 pieces and put in a non-metallic dish. Add the chimichurri (save a little for serving) and toss to coat. Cover and refrigerate for no longer than 3 hours, or the vinegar will start to 'cook' the chicken.

Soak 8 bamboo skewers in water for 1 hour prior to cooking. Remove the chicken from the fridge 20 minutes before cooking and thread 3–4 pieces of meat onto each skewer. Reserve the marinade and put the skewers on a tray.

Your firepit is ready to cook on after about 2 hours of burning, when the timber is charcoal black, has transformed into red hot coals about the size of golf balls, and the smoke has all but subsided. To test for heat, you should not be able to hold the palm of your hand 5–10 cm (2–4 inches) above the grill for more than 2–3 seconds. Replace the grill over the firepit and give it around 10 minutes to heat up. (See page 9.)

Put the chicken skewers on the grill and cook for about 12 minutes until golden brown, brushing with marinade and turning so each side cooks for 3 minutes. Serve with lemon wedges and a little extra chimichurri on the side.

BLACKENED BIRD

This is the classic Cajun spice rub — a favourite in America's southern states. The dark colour comes from the spices being burnt. Always use chicken with the skin on for this — it is the skin, rubbed with spices, that absorbs the intense firepit heat.

SERVES 4

2 spatchcock (small chickens), about 500 g (1 lb 2 oz) each

Lime wedges, to serve

CAJUN RUB

2 tablespoons smoked paprika

1 teaspoon dried oregano

1 teaspoon dried thyme

¼ teaspoon cayenne pepper

2 teaspoons sea salt flakes

2 garlic cloves, crushed

2 tablespoons light olive oil

Combine the Cajun rub ingredients in a small bowl.

Cut each spatchcock in half through its breastbone. Remove the cartilage in the breastbone and cut off the wing tips. Pat dry with paper towel.

Rub spice blend all over the spatchcock and put the pieces in a snug-fitting non-metallic dish. Refrigerate for at least 3 hours, or overnight if you like.

Remove from the fridge 30 minutes before cooking.

Your firepit is ready to cook on after about 2 hours of burning, when the timber is charcoal black, has transformed into red hot coals about the size of golf balls, and the smoke has all but subsided. To test for heat, you should not be able to hold the palm of your hand 5–10 cm (2–4 inches) above the grill for more than 2–3 seconds. Replace the grill over the firepit and give it around 10 minutes to heat up. (See page 9.)

Lay the spatchcock, skin side down, on the edge of the grill, where the heat is less intense. Cook for 15 minutes. The skin should be darkened with a reddish tone from the paprika. Turn over and cook for a further 15 minutes, or until the chicken is cooked through. Remove to a plate and loosely cover with foil for about 15 minutes, but not too tightly — you don't want them to sweat and the skin to lose its crispiness under there. Serve warm with lime wedges.

QUAIL WITH PEANUT AND THAI HERB PESTO

Big and bold Asian flavours, especially Thai ingredients, make for great marinades, sauces and dressings. These flavours also very much typify modern Australian cooking. This recipe uses lots of exotic herbs, that thrive in our climate, combined with Thai staples that can be bought easily at any local Asian specialty stores and most supermarkets.

SERVES 4

8 jumbo quails, about 200 g (7 oz) each

1 lime, cut in half

1 tablespoon olive oil

1 teaspoon white pepper

1 handful coriander (cilantro), roughly chopped

PEANUT AND THAI HERB PESTO

¼ cup (40 g) crushed peanuts

2 garlic cloves, chopped

1 teaspoon white pepper

1 large green chilli, chopped

1 small bunch Thai basil leaves

1 small bunch coriander (cilantro), leaves only

1 small bunch mint leaves, roughly chopped

1 tablespoon fish sauce

1 teaspoon sugar

1 tablespoon lime juice

1 tablespoon olive oil

To make the pesto, put all the ingredients in a food processor and whiz to a chunky paste. Cover and refrigerate until needed. This can be made several hours in advance — any longer, and it will lose its distinctive zingy freshness.

To prepare the quails, put on a chopping board, breast side up. Hold the bird with one hand and insert a heavy, sharp knife into the cavity, firmly cutting either side of the backbone all the way through. Throw the backbone away and spread the quail open on the chopping board with the skin side up. Press firmly down on the breast with the palm of your hand to flatten the bird. Repeat with the other quails. Wash the quails and pat dry. Now gently separate the skin from the flesh, being careful not to tear the skin.

Reserve ¼ cup of the Thai pesto and set aside. Spoon some of the remaining pesto under the quail skin and gently spread over the breast and as far down towards the leg as you can, without tearing the skin. Squeeze the lime over the skin of the quails and set aside for 20 minutes.

Your firepit is ready to cook on after about 2 hours of burning, when the timber is charcoal black, has transformed into red hot coals about the size of golf balls, and the smoke has all but subsided. To test for heat, you should not be able to hold the palm of your hand 5—10 cm (2—4 inches) above the grill for more than 2—3 seconds. Replace the grill over the firepit and give it around 10 minutes to heat up. (See page 9.)

Put a baking tray on the firepit grill and allow 10 minutes or so to heat up. Drizzle the olive oil over the tray. Put the quail, skin side down, on the tray and cook for 8—10 minutes, or until the skin is golden. Turn and cook for another 10 minutes. Remove to a plate, loosely cover with foil and leave for 5 minutes. Sprinkle with white pepper and coriander and serve with the reserved pesto.

LEBANESE CHICKEN WITH TOUM

Trim the fat off the chicken thighs if you must, but I would encourage you to leave it on. Most of it will render off as it cooks, but it acts as a buffer between the thigh meat and the intense heat of the firepit, leaving the thigh tender and very tasty. The real star here is the toum, or garlic cream. This is the toothsome stuff you most definitely would find at any good Lebanese restaurant. It has no yolks — just egg whites — and tastes so bloody good.

SERVES 4

6 large skinless boneless chicken thighs

½ cup (125 ml) lemon juice

½ cup (125 ml) white wine

2 teaspoons sea salt

1 teaspoon sugar

1 teaspoon dried oregano

1 small handful flat-leaf (Italian) parsley leaves

TOUM

4 garlic cloves, chopped

2 egg whites

¾ cup (185 ml) olive oil

Make the toum by mixing together the garlic and egg whites in a food processor. With the motor running, slowly add the olive oil until the mixture is fluffy, white and creamy. Transfer to a bowl. Cover and refrigerate until needed. This can be made several hours in advance.

Combine the chicken, lemon juice, white wine, sea salt, sugar and oregano in a non-metallic bowl. Set aside at room temperature for 30 minutes, or cover and refrigerate for 3–6 hours. Remove from the fridge 30 minutes before cooking.

Your firepit is ready to cook on after about 2 hours of burning, when the timber is charcoal black, has transformed into red hot coals about the size of golf balls, and the smoke has all but subsided. To test for heat, you should not be able to hold the palm of your hand 5–10 cm (2–4 inches) above the grill for more than 2–3 seconds. Replace the grill over the firepit and give it around 10 minutes to heat up. (See page 9.)

Put the chicken on the firepit grill and cook for 8 minutes. Turn and cook for another 5 minutes, until cooked through. Sprinkle with parsley and serve with toum.

FESTIVE TURKEY

For this treat, Christmastime or not, you will probably have to order a boneless turkey breast roll from your butcher. This will be the real deal: unprocessed and without any added flavourings. The rule of thumb for cooking turkey is 40 minutes for every kilo, plus an extra 20 minutes. As this is not being cooked in the oven, the timing is a bit different. Season the turkey well and don't overcook. Those are two simple rules to follow for a lovely piece of meat.

SERVES 4

1 boneless turkey breast roll, about 1.6 kg (3 lb 8 oz), skin on

1 tablespoon olive oil

1 tablespoon sea salt

1 teaspoon freshly ground black pepper

1 small handful toasted flaked almonds

SALSA VERDE

1 bunch flat-leaf (Italian) parsley, chopped

24 basil leaves

2 anchovies, chopped

2 teaspoons salted capers, rinsed and drained

½ cup (125 ml) olive oil

1 tablespoon lemon juice

Remove any wrapping the turkey came in. Rub the skin all over with the oil and sit on a chopping board. Sprinkle with the salt and pepper. Leave for 1 hour prior to cooking. Cover with a clean tea towel if you like.

Your firepit is ready to cook on after about 2 hours of burning, when the timber is charcoal black, has transformed into red hot coals about the size of golf balls, and the smoke has all but subsided. To test for heat, you should not be able to hold the palm of your hand 5–10 cm (2–4 inches) above the grill for more than 2–3 seconds. Replace the grill over the firepit and give it around 10 minutes to heat up. (See page 9.)

Put the turkey on the firepit, skin side down. Cook for 8–10 minutes, until the skin is nicely browned all over. Move the turkey around if the skin is starting to catch and burn. Turn over and cook for a further 10 minutes.

Transfer the turkey to a disposable aluminium baking tray. Put another tray on top and fold the edges together to enclose the turkey. Sit the tray on the side of the firepit grill, where it isn't too hot, and cook for 1 hour 15 minutes. After 1 hour, have a peek inside and look at the underside of the turkey. If it is starting to catch or brown too much, move the tray to the furthest edge of the firepit, so it retains heat and continues to cook without burning. Transfer to a chopping board and rest for 45 minutes.

Make the salsa verde while the turkey is resting. Put the parsley in a food processor with the basil, anchovies and capers. Process for a few seconds to finely chop. With the motor running, add the olive oil until well combined. Transfer to a bowl and stir in the lemon juice. Taste for seasoning.

Carve the turkey and arrange on a serving plate. Spoon salsa verde over the top and scatter with almonds to serve.

SPICED QUAIL WITH VIETNAMESE LIME AND PEPPER DIPPING SAUCE

Every Vietnamese restaurant seems to have its own version of this quail: probably marinated and then deep-fried. Here, I am going for grilling over the firepit. The dipping sauce is zesty and peppery, with a sherbet-like feel on the tongue.

SERVES 4

8 quails

1 tablespoon rice bran oil

½ teaspoon Chinese five-spice

1 teaspoon sea salt

Lime wedges, to serve

LIME AND PEPPER SAUCE

3 tablespoons lime juice

½ teaspoon ground white pepper

½ teaspoon caster (superfine) sugar

To make the lime and pepper sauce, combine all the ingredients in a small bowl.

Sit each quail on a chopping board, breast side up. Insert a small sharp knife into the cavity of the quail and cut either side of the backbone. Remove and discard the backbone. Open the quail to flatten on the chopping board, so it is butterflied. Using the palm of your hand, press down on the breastbone to flatten.

Cut each quail in half lengthways and put in a large bowl with the rice bran oil, five-spice and sea salt, tossing to coat. Set aside for 1 hour.

Your firepit is ready to cook on after about 2 hours of burning, when the timber is charcoal black, has transformed into red hot coals about the size of golf balls, and the smoke has all but subsided. To test for heat, you should not be able to hold the palm of your hand 5–10 cm (2–4 inches) above the grill for more than 2–3 seconds. Replace the grill over the firepit and give it around 10 minutes to heat up. (See page 9.)

Put the quails on the firepit grill and cook for 10 minutes. If the quails are starting to burn, move to the edge of the firepit where the heat is less intense. Turn and cook for another 4–5 minutes, until golden and cooked through.

Serve the quails with the lime and pepper sauce on the side, and the lime wedges.

TERIYAKI AND BEER CHICKEN

The Japanese are the masters of really tasty grilled food. Yet their flavourings are subtle. The beer is not a traditional Japanese marinade ingredient, but I couldn't resist using it to add extra flavour to my favourite cut of chicken, the tender thigh.

SERVES 4

8 boneless chicken thighs

TERIYAKI AND BEER SAUCE

4 tablespoons beer (a light ale is good here, preferably Japanese)

4 tablespoons Japanese soy sauce

1 tablespoon sugar

1 teaspoon mustard powder

To make the teriyaki and beer sauce, mix the ingredients in a small bowl and stir until the sugar has dissolved.

Put the chicken in a flat non-metallic dish and pour in the marinade. Cover and refrigerate for no more than 3 hours, turning the chicken often. Remove from the fridge 20 minutes before cooking.

Your firepit is ready to cook on after about 2 hours of burning, when the timber is charcoal black, has transformed into red hot coals about the size of golf balls, and the smoke has all but subsided. To test for heat, you should not be able to hold the palm of your hand 5–10 cm (2–4 inches) above the grill for more than 2–3 seconds. Replace the grill over the firepit and give it around 10 minutes to heat up. (See page 9.)

Put the chicken thighs on the grill, reserving the marinade, and cook for 8 minutes. Turn over and cook for a further 5 minutes. Now start basting with the teriyaki and beer sauce, turning the chicken every minute. Continue for about 4 minutes, until the edges of the thighs are starting to look slightly charred and the rest of the chicken is a dark amber colour. Remove to a plate, loosely cover with foil and rest for 5 minutes before serving.

LEMON CHICKEN, FETA AND HERB ROLLS

This is an Italian thing — rolling a flattened piece of meat, usually veal, into a log and flavouring it. I had to have an excuse to include soft marinated feta in a recipe in this book, so here it is! These involtini are thick buggers, so don't rush the cooking: let them sizzle gently and slowly. The grilled rolls are put into a baking tray and back onto the grill to ensure you don't lose any of those delicious pan juices.

SERVES 4

4 large skinless boneless chicken thighs

¼ cup (35 g) soft feta cheese (marinated or Persian feta)

4 short rosemary sprigs

2 tablespoons olive oil

2 tablespoons lemon juice

1 handful flat-leaf (Italian) parsley leaves, roughly chopped

2 tablespoons chopped oregano leaves

Put each chicken thigh between two layers of plastic wrap and gently pound to an even thickness all over, about 5 mm (¼ inch). Spread 1 tablespoon feta over each flattened thigh and put a sprig of rosemary across. Gently roll up the thigh from one short end, enclosing the feta and rosemary so it sticks out at either end. Tie the involtini with kitchen string and put in a non-metallic dish.

Combine the olive oil, lemon juice and remaining herbs in a bowl and pour over the chicken. Cover and refrigerate for at least 3 hours.

Remove the involtini from the fridge 20 minutes before cooking. Tear off a sheet of foil to cover a baking tray then tear off a similar-sized sheet of baking paper and lay on top of the foil.

Your firepit is ready to cook on after about 2 hours of burning, when the timber is charcoal black, has transformed into red hot coals about the size of golf balls, and the smoke has all but subsided. To test for heat, you should not be able to hold the palm of your hand 5–10 cm (2–4 inches) above the grill for more than 2–3 seconds. Replace the grill over the firepit and give it around 10 minutes to heat up. (See page 9.)

Put the involtini on the edge of the firepit grill and cook for 16–18 minutes, turning often so they sizzle the whole time and are golden brown all over. Transfer the chicken to the prepared tray. Scrunch the sides of the foil to loosely enclose the chicken. Sit the tray on the edge of the firepit and cook for a further 10 minutes. This will ensure the chicken is cooked through and the juices are caught in the tray. Leave to rest for 10 minutes before serving.

PIRI PIRI SPATCHCOCK

We have seen many fast-food franchises claiming to provide authentic Portuguese-flavoured grilled chicken. Some of it is very good. My version of piri piri makes a similar claim by title, although it is by no means traditional, with the inclusion of Chinese chilli garlic sauce and shop-bought roasted red capsicum in the ingredient list. But I think it is very tasty and extremely easy — perfect for the firepit.

SERVES 6

4 spatchcock (small chickens), about 500 g (1 lb 2 oz) each

PIRI PIRI MARINADE

300 g (10½ oz) chopped shop-bought roasted red capsicum (pepper)

4 tablespoons Chinese chilli garlic sauce

1½ tablespoons olive oil

1½ teaspoons ground cumin

1½ teaspoons fresh marjoram, plus extra, for serving

To make the piri piri marinade, put all the ingredients in a food processor and blend until smooth.

Sit each spatchcock, breast side up, on a chopping board. Lay the palm of your hand on the top to hold it stable. Insert a large knife into the cavity and cut down either side of the backbone. Remove and discard the backbone.

Flatten the spatchcock on the chopping board by firmly pressing down on the breastbone with the palm of your hand.

Put the spatchcock in a large dish and rub all over with two-thirds of the marinade. Refrigerate the remaining marinade until needed. Cover the spatchcock and refrigerate for 3–6 hours or overnight, turning often. Remove from the fridge 30 minutes before cooking and sprinkle with sea salt.

Your firepit is ready to cook on after about 2 hours of burning, when the timber is charcoal black, has transformed into red hot coals about the size of golf balls, and the smoke has all but subsided. To test for heat, you should not be able to hold the palm of your hand 5–10 cm (2–4 inches) above the grill for more than 2–3 seconds. Replace the grill over the firepit and give it around 10 minutes to heat up. (See page 9.)

Lay the spatchcock, skin side down, on the firepit grill and cook for 10–15 minutes, until aromatic and the skin is dark golden. Turn over and cook for another 10 minutes. Move to the edge of the firepit, where the heat is less intense. Leave for 10–15 minutes, until cooked through. Insert a knife into the thickest part of the bird — the juices should run clear.

Scatter with fresh marjoram leaves and serve with the reserved marinade as a sauce.

FIREPIT CHICKEN WITH GREEN OLIVE SALSA VERDE

Salsa verde can be simply translated to 'green sauce'. Purists would not include green olives here. If you're not an olive fan, you can leave them out and include some more capers instead. This sauce really needs the tang of the brine mixture (which are what capers and olives are preserved in) to complement the fresh herbs and balance the oil.

SERVES 6—8

Two 1.25 kg (2 lb 12 oz) chickens

3 tablespoons olive oil

3 tablespoons lemon juice

GREEN OLIVE SALSA VERDE

1 thick slice white bread, crusts removed

½ cup (60 g) pitted green olives

1 large handful flat-leaf (Italian) parsley leaves, chopped

1 large handful mint leaves, chopped

1 large handful celery leaves, chopped

1 tablespoon salted capers, well rinsed

2 garlic cloves, chopped

2 anchovies

2 tablespoons lemon juice

3 tablespoons olive oil

Cut the chickens in half through the breastbone, remove the cartilage and backbone, and cut off the wing tips. Pat dry with paper towel.

Put the chickens in a large bowl. Add the olive oil and lemon juice, and rub all over the chickens. Season with sea salt and black pepper and set aside for at least 20 minutes. The chicken can be prepared 6—12 hours in advance, covered and stored in the fridge. Remove from the fridge 30 minutes before cooking.

For the green olive salsa verde, tear the bread and put in a food processor with the olives, herbs, celery leaves, capers, garlic, anchovies and lemon juice. Pulse to combine, leaving the mixture a little chunky. Put into a bowl and stir through the olive oil. Season with black pepper.

Your firepit is ready to cook on after about 2 hours of burning, when the timber is charcoal black, has transformed into red hot coals about the size of golf balls, and the smoke has all but subsided. To test for heat, you should not be able to hold the palm of your hand 5—10 cm (2—4 inches) above the grill for more than 2—3 seconds. Replace the grill over the firepit and give it around 10 minutes to heat up. (See page 9.)

Put the chickens on the firepit grill, skin side down, and cook for 15—20 minutes, pressing down occasionally with a flat metal spatula, until the skin is dark golden and crispy. Turn and cook for a further 15 minutes. Move the chicken to the edge of the firepit, where the heat is less intense, and leave for 20 minutes until cooked through. Make a small, deep incision between the end of the drumstick and the breast — the juices should run clear. Remove to a plate and loosely cover with foil for 10 minutes to rest. Serve with the salsa verde spooned over the top.

CHILLI YOGHURT CHICKEN

Don't you just love a good food memory? I remember my first banana fritter — yum. And my first taste of coriander — odd and challenging. And this combination of yoghurt and chicken I had at a cutting-edge café in the Blue Mountains, west of Sydney, in the early 1980s. I say cutting edge because the gals who ran this place were exploring flavours and ingredients 10 years ahead of everyone else. When much of the food scene was haute and uptight, they were doing big, bold, tasty food from Asia and the Middle East. They passed on this recipe to me.

SERVES 6

6 skinless boneless
chicken thighs
½ cup (130 g) plain yoghurt
2 garlic cloves, crushed
½ teaspoon ground ginger
¼ teaspoon chilli powder
2 tablespoons lemon juice
Light olive oil, for cooking
Lemon wedges, to serve

Put the chicken on a chopping board. Pound the thick end of the thigh so it becomes even thickness all over.

Combine the yoghurt, garlic, ginger, chilli powder and lemon juice in a large non-metallic bowl. Add the chicken and toss to coat. Cover and refrigerate for 6 hours or overnight.

Remove from the fridge 30 minutes before cooking.

Your firepit is ready to cook on after about 2 hours of burning, when the timber is charcoal black, has transformed into red hot coals about the size of golf balls, and the smoke has all but subsided. To test for heat, you should not be able to hold the palm of your hand 5—10 cm (2—4 inches) above the grill for more than 2—3 seconds. Replace the grill over the firepit and give it around 10 minutes to heat up. (See page 9.)

Put the chicken on the firepit grill and cook for 7—8 minutes until golden. Make sure the chicken sizzles the whole time. If it is starting to burn, move to the edge where the heat is less intense. Turn and cook for another 7—8 minutes, or until cooked through. Serve with lemon wedges.

HARISSA CHICKEN

Harissa takes many forms. This fiery Moroccan condiment looks crazily hot but it does mellow with time. Because it is loaded with dried chillies, it lasts several weeks in the fridge. I struggle to think of anything harissa won't go with. As well as chicken, serve with your favourite beef or lamb sausages, grilled vegetables and seafood.

SERVES 4

12 chicken drumsticks

1 handful coriander (cilantro) leaves, chopped

1 handful flat-leaf (Italian) parsley, chopped

1 tablespoon lemon juice

HARISSA

24 large dried red chillies

4 garlic cloves, chopped

2 teaspoons ground cumin

1 teaspoon ground coriander

1 teaspoon salt

½ cup (125 ml) olive oil

To make the harissa, put the chillies in a heatproof bowl and add enough boiling water to cover. Leave for 1 hour. Drain well. (For a less hot harissa, squeeze out and discard the seeds.) Roughly chop the chillies and put in a food processor with the remaining ingredients. Process for 2–3 minutes to make a fine paste. This can be stored in a container in the fridge for several weeks.

Cut a couple of deep incisions across the skin side of the drumsticks and put them in a bowl. Add 2–3 tablespoons of harissa and rub into the chicken. Cover and refrigerate for 3–6 hours, or overnight if you have time.

Your firepit is ready to cook on after about 2 hours of burning, when the timber is charcoal black, has transformed into red hot coals about the size of golf balls, and the smoke has all but subsided. To test for heat, you should not be able to hold the palm of your hand 5–10 cm (2–4 inches) above the grill for more than 2–3 seconds. Replace the grill over the firepit and give it around 10 minutes to heat up. (See page 9.)

Put the chicken on the firepit grill and let it gently sizzle without turning or moving for 10 minutes. If the chicken is starting to burn, move to the edge where the heat is less intense. Turn and cook for another 8 minutes, again without turning or moving the chicken. The chicken should be golden brown. Transfer to a large bowl, cover with foil and rest for 5 minutes. Add the chopped herbs and lemon juice, toss to coat the chicken and serve.

GREEN CURRY CHICKEN

This isn't a curry exactly, but it does have all the great flavours of a Thai green curry. Again, when cooking chicken, do be patient and remove it from the fridge about 30 minutes before cooking so it comes to room temperature for better flavour.

SERVES 4

800g (1 lb 12 oz) chicken tenderloins

1 tablespoon coconut cream

1 handful Thai basil leaves

Lime wedges, to serve

GREEN CURRY PASTE

1 teaspoon coriander seeds

1 teaspoon cumin seeds

1 teaspoon white peppercorns

2 large green chillies, seeded and chopped

1 lemongrass stalk, chopped

2 garlic cloves, chopped

3 spring onions (scallions), chopped

4 small makrut lime leaves, shredded

1 tablespoon grated ginger

4 coriander (cilantro) roots

1 small handful coriander (cilantro) stems, chopped

1 tablespoon fish sauce

1 tablespoon sugar

3 tablespoons coconut cream

To make the curry paste, put the coriander and cumin seeds and peppercorns in a small frying pan over high heat. Shake the pan until they start to smoke and darken. Remove from the pan and allow to cool. Transfer to a small food processor or spice mill and grind. Add the remaining curry paste ingredients and process in bursts, scraping down the sides of the bowl until you have a chunky, pale green paste.

Put the chicken in a bowl. Rub the paste all over the chicken, cover and refrigerate for 3–6 hours or overnight. Remove from the fridge 30 minutes before cooking.

Your firepit is ready to cook on after about 2 hours of burning, when the timber is charcoal black, has transformed into red hot coals about the size of golf balls, and the smoke has all but subsided. To test for heat, you should not be able to hold the palm of your hand 5–10 cm (2–4 inches) above the grill for more than 2–3 seconds. Replace the grill over the firepit and give it around 10 minutes to heat up. (See page 9.)

Put the chicken on the firepit grill and cook for 10 minutes, turning every couple of minutes, until golden and cooked through. Remove to a serving plate, drizzle with the coconut cream and scatter with Thai basil leaves. Serve with lime wedges on the side.

THAI BARBECUED CHICKEN

If you look at the ingredients in the coriander and pepper rub you could be excused for thinking that it all sounds a bit intense. But that is the nature of Thai cooking. It is all in the balance. A good Thai meal is like a roller coaster of flavours in your mouth — challenging, scary to some, and quite addictive.

SERVES 4

6 skinless boneless chicken thighs

1 small handful coriander (cilantro) sprigs, to serve

Lime wedges, to serve

CORIANDER AND PEPPER RUB

6 coriander (cilantro) roots and stems, chopped

6 garlic cloves, chopped

½ teaspoon black peppercorns

½ teaspoon white peppercorns

3 tablespoons fish sauce

4 spring onions (scallions), chopped

To prepare the chicken thighs, put them on a chopping board, smooth side down (the smooth side is where the skin once was). You should be able to easily see the thicker part of the thigh. Use a small sharp knife to butterfly this part of the thigh, so the thigh is then an even thickness all over.

Put the chicken in a bowl and refrigerate while making the coriander and pepper rub.

Pound the coriander and a pinch of sea salt with a mortar and pestle for a couple of minutes until pulpy, then add the garlic. Pound again until the garlic is also pulpy, then add the remaining rub ingredients. Pound to a chunky paste.

Pour the rub over the chicken. Stir or combine with your hands so the chicken is coated all over in the marinade. Cover and refrigerate for 3—6 hours. Remove from the fridge 30 minutes before cooking.

Your firepit is ready to cook on after about 2 hours of burning, when the timber is charcoal black, has transformed into red hot coals about the size of golf balls, and the smoke has all but subsided. To test for heat, you should not be able to hold the palm of your hand 5—10 cm (2—4 inches) above the grill for more than 2—3 seconds. Replace the grill over the firepit and give it around 10 minutes to heat up. (See page 9.)

Put the chicken on the firepit grill, keeping the marinade. Cook for 8 minutes. Spoon the reserved marinade over the chicken. Turn and cook for a further 5 minutes, pressing down a few times with a flat metal spatula, until the chicken is cooked through. Put on a serving plate, cover with foil and leave to rest for 10 minutes before serving with coriander and lime wedges.

CHICKEN WITH JALAPEÑO BUTTER

A couple of my fave things here — jalapeños in brine and chicken breast with the skin on. It seems we've all become a little obsessed about skinless chicken breasts (and what an odd obsession, don't you think?), but leaving the skin on makes all the difference when it comes to flavour. Even if you don't like the skin (you can always remove it yourself — someone else at the table is bound to snap it up) but leaving it on for cooking keeps the meat lovely and tender. As for jalapeños, I use them all the time in salsas with corn, in mayonnaise and even Chinese stir-fries with pork or duck.

SERVES 4

4 chicken breasts, skin on and and wings attached (supreme or Kiev)

1 tablespoon olive oil

Lime wedges, to serve

1 small handful coriander (cilantro) leaves, to serve

JALAPEÑO BUTTER

2 tablespoons sliced jalapeños in brine, drained

1 garlic clove, chopped

1 large handful coriander (cilantro) leaves

2 anchovy fillets in oil, drained

½ cup (125 g) unsalted butter, softened to room temperature

To make the jalapeño butter, put all the ingredients in a food processor and whiz until well combined.

Rub as much of the butter mixture as you can under the skin of the chicken breasts, being careful not to break the skin. Rub any remaining butter over the skin and sprinkle with a little sea salt. You can secure the skin with toothpicks to keep it in place while it cooks (otherwise it can pull back from the meat).

Your firepit is ready to cook on after about 2 hours of burning, when the timber is charcoal black, has transformed into red hot coals about the size of golf balls, and the smoke has all but subsided. To test for heat, you should not be able to hold the palm of your hand 5–10 cm (2–4 inches) above the grill for more than 2–3 seconds. Replace the grill over the firepit and give it around 10 minutes to heat up. (See page 9.)

Put a baking tray on the firepit grill. Allow 10 minutes for it to heat up. Drizzle the olive oil on the baking tray.

Put the chicken on the tray, skin side down, and cook for 10 minutes, until the skin is golden. Turn over and cook for a further 10 minutes, until cooked through. Transfer to a plate and allow to rest for 10–15 minutes. Serve with lime wedges and coriander.

CHINATOWN DUCK SHANKS

When I first saw the words duck and shank together I thought it must be a mistake, or a joke. After all, isn't a shank part of the leg of a four-legged creature? I was thinking lamb. But, no. Apparently, shank is part of the leg of any vertebrate. Anyway, lucky for me I live but 20 minutes from Australia's largest free-range duck farm. This means lots of whole ducks, livers, marylands and shanks.

SERVES 4

12 duck shanks

2 tablespoons hoisin sauce

2 tablespoons light soy sauce

2 tablespoons Chinese rice wine

2 star anise

2 drops cochineal (optional)

2 tablespoons runny honey

Chinese barbecue sauce
(char siu), to serve

Put the duck shanks in a non-metallic dish with the hoisin sauce, soy sauce, rice wine, star anise and cochineal, if using. Toss the shanks around in the marinade. Cover and refrigerate for 24 hours, turning the duck every 6–8 hours.

Remove from the fridge 30 minutes before cooking.

Your firepit is ready to cook on after about 2 hours of burning, when the timber is charcoal black, has transformed into red hot coals about the size of golf balls, and the smoke has all but subsided. To test for heat, you should not be able to hold the palm of your hand 5–10 cm (2–4 inches) above the grill for more than 2–3 seconds. Replace the grill over the firepit and give it around 10 minutes to heat up. (See page 9.)

Put the duck shanks on the firepit grill. Cook for 20 minutes. If they are starting to cook too quickly and burn, move them to the edge of the firepit where the heat is less intense. Turn the shanks over and cook for another 10 minutes, or until golden. Brush the honey over the shanks and cook for another 5 minutes, turning and brushing each side with honey until they are glistening and crisp.

Arrange on a serving platter and serve with Chinese barbecue sauce on the side.

CHICKEN SHAWARMA

Authentic shawarma has the meat roasted on a vertical spit. No mean feat! Cooking this Levantine Arabic dish on the firepit makes perfect sense. Actually, many of the skewered and grilled meats that typify Middle Eastern cooking translate brilliantly to firepit cooking.

SERVES 4—6

8 skinless boneless chicken thighs

2 red onions, finely sliced

4 tablespoons olive oil

4 tablespoons lemon juice

6 garlic cloves, finely chopped

1 teaspoon ground turmeric

1 teaspoon ground ginger

1 teaspoon chilli powder

1 tablespoon sweet paprika

1 tablespoon ground cumin

1 small handful roughly chopped Italian (flat-leaf) parsley leaves

1 small handful roughly chopped coriander (cilantro)

8 soft pitta breads

250 g (9 oz) plain yoghurt

Lebanese pickles, to serve

To prepare the chicken thighs, put them on a chopping board, smooth side down (the smooth side is where the skin once was). You should be able to easily see the thicker part of the thigh. Use a small sharp knife to butterfly this part of the thigh, so the thigh is then an even thickness all over.

Put the chicken in a bowl with the red onion, lemon juice, garlic, all the spices and parsley. Stir well or, even better, use your hands to combine. Cover and refrigerate for 3—6 hours. Remove from the fridge 30 minutes before cooking.

Your firepit is ready to cook on after about 2 hours of burning, when the timber is charcoal black, has transformed into red hot coals about the size of golf balls, and the smoke has all but subsided. To test for heat, you should not be able to hold the palm of your hand 5—10 cm (2—4 inches) above the grill for more than 2—3 seconds. Replace the grill over the firepit and give it around 10 minutes to heat up. (See page 9.)

Lay the chicken thighs on the firepit grill. Cook for 8 minutes. Turn and cook for a further 5 minutes, until the thickest part of the thigh is cooked through. Remove to a platter and sprinkle with coriander.

Throw the pitta bread onto the grill, turning a couple of times until it is cooked to your liking.

The idea here is that everyone makes their own. Serve the chicken and bread with yoghurt and pickles on the side.

KERALAN CHICKEN

Keralan cuisine is much less complex and full-on than dishes from other parts of India. And by full-on I mean heavy and rich. This is a very simple but delicious barbecued chicken dish. It would also work really well with a chicken maryland (drumstick and thigh on the bone). But if you do cook chicken on the bone, remember it will need a longer cooking time.

SERVES 4

4 boneless chicken breasts, skin on

3 tablespoons lemon juice

2 garlic cloves, finely chopped

1 tablespoon finely grated ginger

1 small onion, chopped

¼ teaspoon ground turmeric

1 teaspoon ground cumin

1 teaspoon sweet paprika

¼ teaspoon chilli powder

Vegetable oil, for cooking

4 slices naan bread or other flatbread

Sliced tomato, red onion, mint, plain yoghurt and lemon wedges, to serve

Put the chicken in a non-metallic dish.

Put the lemon juice, garlic, ginger, onion, turmeric, cumin, paprika and chilli powder in a food processor and process to a smooth paste. Pour over the chicken and roll the chicken around to coat in the marinade. Cover and refrigerate for 6 hours or overnight. Remove from the fridge 30 minutes before cooking.

Your firepit is ready to cook on after about 2 hours of burning, when the timber is charcoal black, has transformed into red hot coals about the size of golf balls, and the smoke has all but subsided. To test for heat, you should not be able to hold the palm of your hand 5–10 cm (2–4 inches) above the grill for more than 2–3 seconds. Replace the grill over the firepit and give it around 10 minutes to heat up. (See page 9.)

Put the chicken, skin side down, on the firepit grill and cook for 8–10 minutes, or until the skin is golden. Turn the chicken over and cook for a further 10 minutes, or until cooked through. Remove to a plate and cover loosely with foil. Rest for 10 minutes before carving.

Cook the bread on the firepit until warmed through and a little charred. Serve slices of chicken on the bread and top with tomato, red onion and mint leaves. Serve with yoghurt and lemon wedges.

COCONUT TENDERLOINS

This is kind of Indian-style, but then again the flavours are more typical of the Caribbean — lots of fragrant spice, coconut and tropical lime. Tenderloins are great, as they don't have the fat of the chicken thigh but don't tend to dry out either.

SERVES 4

800 g (1 lb 12 oz) chicken tenderloins

1 onion, chopped

1 handful flat-leaf (Italian) parsley

1 handful coriander (cilantro)

¼ teaspoon ground cloves

¼ teaspoon ground cinnamon

1 tablespoon lime juice

1 cup (250 ml) coconut milk

2 tablespoons light olive oil

Lime wedges, to serve

½ teaspoon sweet paprika, to serve (optional)

Coriander (cilantro) sprigs, to serve (optional)

Place the chicken tenderloins in a large non-metallic dish.

Put the onion, parsley, coriander, cloves, cinnamon, lime juice and coconut milk in a food processor and process to a paste. Pour over the chicken and toss to coat. Cover and refrigerate for 3–6 hours. Remove from the fridge 30 minutes before cooking.

Your firepit is ready to cook on after about 2 hours of burning, when the timber is charcoal black, has transformed into red hot coals about the size of golf balls, and the smoke has all but subsided. To test for heat, you should not be able to hold the palm of your hand 5–10 cm (2–4 inches) above the grill for more than 2–3 seconds. Replace the grill over the firepit and give it around 10 minutes to heat up. (See page 9.)

Shake any excess marinade off the chicken and put the tenderloins on the firepit grill, making sure there is some space between them. Cook for 8–10 minutes, turning often, until golden, tender and cooked through.

Serve with the lime wedges and sprinkle with paprika and coriander, if you like.

SWEET CHILLI AND GINGER CHICKEN

In recent years sweet chilli sauce has come to sit proudly next to tomato sauce as a kitchen staple — a true sign of our culinary times. It's sweet and sticky and perfect as a marinade base with all its subtly hidden ingredients.

SERVES 4

8 skinless boneless chicken thighs

SWEET CHILLI MARINADE

150 g (5½ oz) Thai sweet chilli sauce

2 tablespoons Chinese rice wine (or dry white wine)

1 tablespoon fish sauce

1 tablespoon finely grated ginger

1 small bunch coriander (cilantro), chopped

Put each chicken thigh between two layers of plastic wrap and gently pound to an even thickness all over, about 5 mm (¼ inch). I like to leave on the little fat that is on the thigh — it will keep the meat really moist while it cooks.

Put the chicken in a non-metallic dish. Combine the marinade ingredients, pour over the chicken and toss well with your hands to coat. Cover and refrigerate for 3–6 hours. Remove from the fridge 20 minutes before cooking.

Your firepit is ready to cook on after about 2 hours of burning, when the timber is charcoal black, has transformed into red hot coals about the size of golf balls, and the smoke has all but subsided. To test for heat, you should not be able to hold the palm of your hand 5–10 cm (2–4 inches) above the grill for more than 2–3 seconds. Replace the grill over the firepit and give it around 10 minutes to heat up. (See page 9.)

Put the chicken on the firepit grill and cook for 5 minutes, gently pressing down occasionally with a flat metal spatula. Turn over and cook for another 3–4 minutes, again pressing down on the meat. Remove to a plate and cover with foil. Rest for 10 minutes before serving.

FIERY CHICKEN CHOPS

Dried chilli oil has become a must-have staple. It's great for drizzling over meat or, as here, used in a marinade. Another bonus is that it is now sold at supermarkets. Look for the brand with the earnest woman on the label; it's not as hot as it looks, so I also add dried chilli flakes for a little more heat. But do try it first and see what you think before adding any extra chilli.

SERVES 4

½ cup (125 ml) dried chilli oil

1 teaspoon dried chilli flakes

1 tablespoon light soy sauce

1 tablespoon lemon juice

1 garlic clove, chopped

12 chicken chops (dark meat of drumstick and thigh), skin removed, or 6 chicken thigh cutlets, skin on and bone in

1 tablespoon chopped dill

Lemon wedges, to serve

Put the chilli oil, chilli flakes, soy sauce, lemon juice and garlic in a food processor and mix to a fiery red paste.

Put the chicken in a bowl and rub all over with the chilli paste. Cover and refrigerate for 3–6 hours. Remove from the fridge 30 minutes before cooking.

Your firepit is ready to cook on after about 2 hours of burning, when the timber is charcoal black, has transformed into red hot coals about the size of golf balls, and the smoke has all but subsided. To test for heat, you should not be able to hold the palm of your hand 5–10 cm (2–4 inches) above the grill for more than 2–3 seconds. Replace the grill over the firepit and give it around 10 minutes to heat up. (See page 9.)

Put the chicken on the grill and cook for 10 minutes. Turn the chicken over and cook for a further 10 minutes, or until cooked through. Transfer to a plate. Scatter with dill and serve with lemon wedges on the side.

CREOLE CHICKEN

This is a versatile one. Both the marinade and sauce would go really nicely with pork fillet or pork chop, rump steak or flank steak, as well as chicken. I can even imagine this working beautifully with lamb.

SERVES 4

4 boneless chicken breasts, skin on

1 onion, chopped

2 garlic cloves, chopped

1 tablespoon finely chopped coriander (cilantro) stems

2 tablespoons olive oil

2 tablespoons white wine vinegar

SAUCE

2 tablespoons olive oil

2 tablespoons lime juice

2 teaspoons ground cumin

2 garlic cloves, crushed

3 tablespoons chopped coriander (cilantro) leaves

Put the chicken in a non-metallic dish or bowl. Put the onion, garlic, coriander stems, olive oil and vinegar in a food processor and process to a paste. Rub all over the chicken. Cover and refrigerate for 6 hours or overnight. Remove from the fridge 30 minutes before cooking.

To make the sauce, put all the sauce ingredients in a small bowl and stir to combine.

Your firepit is ready to cook on after about 2 hours of burning, when the timber is charcoal black, has transformed into red hot coals about the size of golf balls, and the smoke has all but subsided. To test for heat, you should not be able to hold the palm of your hand 5–10 cm (2–4 inches) above the grill for more than 2–3 seconds. Replace the grill over the firepit and give it around 10 minutes to heat up. (See page 9.)

Put the chicken on the firepit grill, skin side down, and cook for 8–10 minutes. Turn over and cook for another 5 minutes, or until cooked through. Remove and allow to rest for 10 minutes.

Spoon the sauce over the hot chicken to serve.

MERGUEZ SAUSAGES WITH HARISSA 66

T-BONES WITH CAFÉ DE PARIS BUTTER 69

LAMB KEBABS WITH SPICED YOGHURT 70

FRAGRANT BEEF KEFTA 73

HAGEN'S PORK NECK 74

PORK CARNITAS 77

PENANG BEEF SATAY 78

VEAL AND PROVOLONE INVOLTINI 79

LEMONGRASS, PEPPER AND CORIANDER PORK SKEWERS 80

SPICY BEEF KEBABS 83

SMOKY PORK KEBABS 84

LAMB WITH FETA, LEMON AND OREGANO 87

LAMB WITH BASIL PESTO 88

VEAL CUTLETS WITH ROSEMARY, ANCHOVIES AND RED WINE 91

SHEFTALIA 92

LAMB CHOPS WITH ANCHOVY BUTTER 93

ROAST BEEF FILLET WITH PAPRIKA MAYONNAISE 94

CHINATOWN PORK 97

RUMP STEAK WITH GINGER, GARLIC AND SOY 98

MIXED MEAT GRILL 101

LAMB WITH GREEN OLIVE SALSA 102

BUTTERFLIED LAMB MASALA 104

BEEF RIB-EYE WITH HORSERADISH BUTTER 105

NEW YORK COWBOY 107

CHAR SIU LAMB WRAPS 108

BEEF, PORK AND LAMB

MERGUEZ SAUSAGES WITH HARISSA

Made with beef or lamb, these little home-made sausages hail from North Africa. The paprika gives them their unique redness. The harissa can be made in advance: it will keep in the fridge for several weeks and the flavour improves with time.

SERVES 4

750 g (1 lb 10 oz) minced (ground) beef

2 garlic cloves, finely chopped

1 tablespoon ground cumin

2 teaspoons ground coriander

1 tablespoon za'atar mix, plus extra, to serve

1 tablespoon smoked paprika

1 teaspoon cayenne pepper

1 teaspoon dried thyme

1 teaspoon sea salt

Olive oil

HARISSA

24 large dried red chillies

4 garlic cloves, chopped

2 teaspoons ground cumin

1 teaspoon ground coriander

1 teaspoon salt

½ cup (125 ml) olive oil

To make the sausages, put the meat, spices and salt in a large bowl. Use your hands to combine, throwing the meat against the side of the bowl. Lightly grease your hands with olive oil and form the meat into 16 balls about the size of a large walnut. Form each into a small sausage 5–6 cm (2 inches) long. Put them on a tray lined with baking paper. Cover and refrigerate overnight.

To make the harissa, put the chillies in a heatproof bowl and add enough boiling water to cover. Leave for 1 hour. Drain well. (For a less hot harissa, squeeze out and discard the seeds.) Roughly chop the chillies and put in a food processor with the remaining ingredients. Process for 2–3 minutes to make a fine paste. This can be stored in a container in the fridge for several weeks.

Your firepit is ready to cook on after about 2 hours of burning, when the timber is charcoal black, has transformed into red hot coals about the size of golf balls, and the smoke has all but subsided. To test for heat, you should not be able to hold the palm of your hand 5–10 cm (2–4 inches) above the grill for more than 2–3 seconds. Replace the grill over the firepit and give it around 10 minutes to heat up. (See page 9.)

Lightly brush the sausages with olive oil. Put on the firepit grill and cook for 10 minutes, turning every 2 minutes or so, until the meat is no longer pink. These are quite small so once they look cooked all over they will be ready. Serve with the harissa and a sprinkling of za'atar.

T-BONES WITH CAFÉ DE PARIS BUTTER

Compound butter is the cheffy term given to butter that has been flavoured with all sorts of tasty comestibles. The flavoured butter melts on the cooked food and pretty much turns into a sauce. These butters can be made a day or two in advance, and kept in the fridge, leaving them ready to go whenever you fire up your firepit. Some people consider café de Paris butter to be the ultimate addition to a steak.

SERVES 4

4 thick T-bone steaks, about 400 g (14 oz) each

2 garlic cloves, halved

1 tablespoon olive oil

CAFÉ DE PARIS BUTTER

1 tablespoon mild mustard

2 teaspoons Worcestershire sauce

2 tablespoons tomato ketchup

1 garlic clove

1 tablespoon capers, rinsed

6 anchovies

2 tablespoons chopped flat-leaf (Italian) parsley

2 teaspoons thyme leaves

1 teaspoon Madras curry powder

250 g (9 oz) butter, softened

To make the café de Paris butter, put all the ingredients except the butter in a food processor and whiz to a chunky paste. Add the butter and mix to combine. Turn out onto a piece of plastic wrap on a work surface. Firmly wrap and roll to form a log and twist the ends to seal. Refrigerate until the butter is needed.

Rub both sides of the steaks, including the bones, with the cut side of the garlic cloves. Lightly brush the steaks with oil, season with sea salt and freshly ground black pepper and set aside on a tray for 30 minutes.

Your firepit is ready to cook on after about 2 hours of burning, when the timber is charcoal black, has transformed into red hot coals about the size of golf balls, and the smoke has all but subsided. To test for heat, you should not be able to hold the palm of your hand 5–10 cm (2–4 inches) above the grill for more than 2–3 seconds. Replace the grill over the firepit and give it around 10 minutes to heat up. (See page 9.)

Lay the steaks on the firepit grill. Cook for 4 minutes each side for rare, or longer if you prefer.

Transfer the steaks to a plate, cover loosely with foil and rest for 5 minutes. Serve topped with thick slices of the café de Paris butter.

LAMB KEBABS
WITH SPICED YOGHURT

Lamb meat is perfect for barbecuing. However, keep in mind that the lamb leg, much like the rump cut in beef, is made up of several different muscles, so it will vary in texture and tenderness.

SERVES 6

1 small boned leg of lamb, about 1.25 kg (2 lb 12 oz)

3 tablespoons plain yoghurt

1 teaspoon ground cumin

1 teaspoon ground turmeric

½ teaspoon garam masala

2 teaspoons sea salt

1 white onion, chopped

2 garlic cloves, chopped

1 tablespoon finely grated ginger

1 large handful chopped coriander (cilantro) leaves

Olive oil

Lemon wedges, to serve

Cut the lamb into large bite-sized pieces and put in a large non-metallic bowl.

Put the yoghurt, spices, salt, onion, garlic, ginger and coriander in a food processor and mix to a paste. Spoon over the lamb and toss to coat the meat. Cover and refrigerate for 6 hours. Remove from the fridge 1 hour before cooking.

Your firepit is ready to cook on after about 2 hours of burning, when the timber is charcoal black, has transformed into red hot coals about the size of golf balls, and the smoke has all but subsided. To test for heat, you should not be able to hold the palm of your hand 5–10 cm (2–4 inches) above the grill for more than 2–3 seconds. Replace the grill over the firepit and give it around 10 minutes to heat up. (See page 9.)

Thread the lamb onto 6 long metal skewers, or soaked bamboo skewers, and brush with olive oil. Cook on the firepit grill for 20 minutes, turning every 3–4 minutes. Serve with the lemon wedges.

FRAGRANT BEEF KEFTA

Kefta are meatballs in Morocco. These can be grilled, as we've done here, or cooked in a tomato-based sauce and baked in a pot, which could be called a tagine. Ras-el-hanout is a blend of spices, and can vary greatly, somewhat like garam masala in Indian cooking. The beef mixture can be wrapped around metal or bamboo skewers for easy cooking on the firepit. Simply pull the meat off the skewers before serving.

SERVES 4

750 g (1 lb 10 oz) minced (ground) beef

1 red onion, finely chopped

2 garlic cloves, crushed

1 teaspoon ground ginger

2 teaspoons ground cinnamon

2 teaspoons ras-el-hanout (Moroccan spice blend)

1 teaspoon sea salt, plus extra, for seasoning

3 tablespoons finely chopped coriander (cilantro) leaves

3 tablespoons finely chopped flat-leaf (Italian) parsley

3 tablespoons olive oil

Put the beef, onion, garlic, ginger, cinnamon, ras-el-hanout, salt, coriander and parsley in a large bowl. Use your hands to combine. Pick the mince up and firmly throw it back into the bowl, to remove any air and to tenderise the meat. Cover and refrigerate for 2–6 hours.

Using wet hands, divide the mixture in half. Keep dividing in half until you have 16 portions, roughly about the same size. Again, with wet hands, form each portion into a torpedo shape, tapering at each end. Insert a metal or soaked bamboo skewer through each kefta.

Your firepit is ready to cook on after about 2 hours of burning, when the timber is charcoal black, has transformed into red hot coals about the size of golf balls, and the smoke has all but subsided. To test for heat, you should not be able to hold the palm of your hand 5–10 cm (2–4 inches) above the grill for more than 2–3 seconds. Replace the grill over the firepit and give it around 10 minutes to heat up. (See page 9.)

Brush the olive oil over the meat. Put the kefta on the firepit grill, sprinkle with sea salt and cook for 5 minutes without turning or moving. This allows the kefta to form a golden crust so they can then be turned without breaking up. Turn over and cook for another 3–4 minutes until ready.

Best served with toasted pitta bread and a tomato and cucumber salad.

HAGEN'S PORK NECK

I was a tad envious when my friend Hagen made this fantastic meal on a barbecue that was nothing more than a metal drum topped with a grill. Such makeshift cooking devices are sometimes the best and can yield great-tasting food.

SERVES 8

2 kg (4 lb 8 oz) pork neck, butterflied to a thickness of 3–4 cm (1½ inches)

1 bunch coriander (cilantro), finely chopped

8 garlic cloves, roughly chopped

6 large red chillies, chopped

1 teaspoon sea salt

3 tablespoons honey

3 tablespoons dark soy sauce

3 tablespoons Chinese black vinegar

3 tablespoons vegetable oil

Put the pork in a non-metallic dish.

Put the remaining ingredients in a food processor and process to a smooth paste. Rub all over the pork, cover and set aside at room temperature for 2–3 hours, or refrigerate overnight. Remove from the fridge 1 hour before cooking.

Your firepit is ready to cook on after about 2 hours of burning, when the timber is charcoal black, has transformed into red hot coals about the size of golf balls, and the smoke has all but subsided. To test for heat, you should not be able to hold the palm of your hand 5–10 cm (2–4 inches) above the grill for more than 2–3 seconds. Replace the grill over the firepit and give it around 10 minutes to heat up. (See page 9.)

Lay the pork on the firepit grill. Cook for 8–10 minutes each side, until well browned.

Wrap the pork in cooking foil. Return to the firepit, near the edge where the heat is less intense. Cook for 20 minutes. Remove from the grill and leave wrapped in the foil to rest for 20 minutes before carving.

PORK CARNITAS

This recipe involves cooking the pork in a seemingly unusual combination of ingredients. Yet, cooking pork in milk is not unusual in many Latin-based cultures. Here, the milk is deliciously flavoured with bay leaf, oregano, cumin and orange. There are two steps to this: you will need to cook the pork first in a slow cooker or low oven for many hours. The 'pulled' meat is then wrapped in cooking foil so it can easily be reheated on your firepit. This is also a good recipe to have in your repertoire if you are ever asked to 'bring a plate' — it can be easily transported and reheated on someone else's firepit. Have carnitas, will travel.

SERVES 4

1 cup (250 ml) milk

½ cup (125 ml) freshly squeezed orange juice

3 tablespoons light brown sugar

1 tablespoon dried oregano

1 tablespoon ground cumin

1 teaspoon dried chilli flakes

1 bay leaf

1 onion, roughly sliced

3 garlic cloves, roughly chopped

1.25 kg (2 lb 12 oz) piece of pork scotch fillet

8 large soft burritos, to serve

Combine the milk, juice, sugar, oregano, cumin, chilli, bay, onion and garlic in a bowl. Season well with salt and black pepper. Add the pork. Roll the pork around in the marinade.

Put the pork and milk mixture in a slow cooker. Cover and turn the heat to high. Cook for 3 hours. Turn over and cook for a further 3 hours, until the pork easily falls apart when pressed with a fork. (If you don't have a slow cooker, cook in a heavy casserole dish, covered, in a 140°C (285°C) oven for 5 hours.) Switch off and leave in the cooker to cool for 30 minutes.

Use a potato masher to press down gently on the meat — it should fall apart. Use forks to shred any larger pieces of meat. Transfer to a container and refrigerate overnight.

Lay a large sheet of cooking foil on the work surface. Top with a sheet of baking paper. Put the pork on the baking paper, spreading it out slightly. Top with another sheet of baking paper then cooking foil. Fold in the sides to make a parcel.

Your firepit is ready to cook on after about 2 hours of burning, when the timber is charcoal black, has transformed into red hot coals about the size of golf balls, and the smoke has all but subsided. To test for heat, you should not be able to hold the palm of your hand 5—10 cm (2—4 inches) above the grill for more than 2—3 seconds. Replace the grill over the firepit and give it around 10 minutes to heat up. (See page 9.)

Put the pork parcel on the firepit grill and cook for 15—20 minutes, until heated through. Heat the burritos on the grill until golden. Unwrap the meat at the table. Serve with warm burritos.

PENANG BEEF SATAY

Some recipes stand out. I first made this some time ago while researching traditional southern Thai and northern Malay satay sauces. Several recipes had condensed milk listed in the ingredients. Sounds odd, right? But it turns out to be authentic. The sweetness of the milk caramelises, making this a rich affair, so I think it really needs the home-made chilli sauce, spiked with lots of vinegar, drizzled over the top to cut through it. This is possibly — maybe — the best beef satay ever.

SERVES 4 AS A STARTER

400 g (14 oz) beef rump steak

Nam jim, page 192, to serve

PENANG SATAY MARINADE

4 spring onions (scallions), white part only, chopped

½ cup (75 g) crushed peanuts

2 tablespoons curry powder

½ cup (125 ml) condensed milk

½ cup (125 ml) coconut cream

2 tablespoons fish sauce

½ teaspoon turmeric

2 tablespoons brown sugar

To make the Penang satay marinade, put all the ingredients in a food processor and whiz to make a runny, yellowish marinade. Pour into a non-metallic dish.

Put the beef on a chopping board and slice on an angle across the grain into thin strips. Put the beef into the satay marinade, separate the pieces and massage the marinade into the meat. Cover and refrigerate for 3–6 hours or overnight if you have the time. Remove from the fridge 1 hour before cooking.

You will need 16 metal or soaked bamboo skewers. Thread 2–3 pieces of meat onto each skewer. Keep the marinade.

Your firepit is ready to cook on after about 2 hours of burning, when the timber is charcoal black, has transformed into red hot coals about the size of golf balls, and the smoke has all but subsided. To test for heat, you should not be able to hold the palm of your hand 5–10 cm (2–4 inches) above the grill for more than 2–3 seconds. Replace the grill over the firepit and give it around 10 minutes to heat up. (See page 9.)

Put the satay sticks on the firepit grill and cook for 4 minutes, brushing a little remaining marinade onto the beef. These cook quickly. You may need to move the skewers to the edge of the firepit where the heat is less intense, so they don't burn. The cooked side should develop a dark golden crust. Turn over and cook for another 3–4 minutes.

Remove to a platter and serve with nam jim.

VEAL AND PROVOLONE INVOLTINI

Think of involtini as a roll or a log. Provolone is a firm, tasty Italian cheese that melts to a very gooey goodness. This, with the pancetta, really complements the mildly flavoured, yet tender, veal.

SERVES 4

400 g (14 oz) veal backstrap fillet

1 egg, lightly beaten

1 tablespoon finely chopped flat-leaf (Italian) parsley

1 tablespoon finely chopped rosemary

4 slices pancetta

75 g (2½ oz) provolone cheese, thinly sliced

2 tablespoons olive oil

Cut the veal into 4 equal-sized portions. Put the veal between 2 layers of plastic wrap or baking paper and pound until very thin.

Combine the egg, parsley and rosemary and brush over the top of each slice of veal. Top each piece of veal with a slice of pancetta and a layer of provolone.

Firmly roll up the veal into a log and tie with cooking string. Lay the rolls in a tray and rub all over with olive oil. Season with salt and black pepper and set aside for 30 minutes.

Your firepit is ready to cook on after about 2 hours of burning, when the timber is charcoal black, has transformed into red hot coals about the size of golf balls, and the smoke has all but subsided. To test for heat, you should not be able to hold the palm of your hand 5—10 cm (2—4 inches) above the grill for more than 2—3 seconds. Replace the grill over the firepit and give it around 10 minutes to heat up. (See page 9.)

Put the involtini on the firepit grill. Cook for 10 minutes, turning every 2 minutes, until brown all over. Wrap each of the involtini in cooking foil. Return to the firepit, near the edge where the heat is less intense, and cook for a further 15 minutes, until cooked through. Remove and rest for 10 minutes. Slice each roll into 3—4 pieces to serve.

LEMONGRASS, PEPPER AND CORIANDER PORK SKEWERS

In Vietnam and much of Southeast Asia, pork is often used with a combination of sweet, salty and sour flavours. Much of the food is cooked roadside or in market places on mini firepits. Nuoc cham is the generic term for a sauce that combines a few key ingredients to make it pungent, sweet, sour and spicy all at once.

SERVES 4

500 g (1 lb 2 oz) minced (ground) pork

2 lemongrass stalks, white part only, finely chopped

1 teaspoon caster (superfine) sugar

1 tablespoon fish sauce

2 tablespoons chopped coriander (cilantro) roots

1 teaspoon freshly ground black pepper

8 lemongrass stalks, about 15 cm (6 in) long

Olive oil, for brushing

NUOC CHAM

4 small red chillies, finely chopped

2 garlic cloves, finely chopped

2 teaspoons sugar

1 tablespoon rice vinegar

½ cup (125 ml) fish sauce

To make nuoc cham, combine all the ingredients in a bowl.

Put the pork, chopped lemongrass, sugar, fish sauce, coriander and black pepper in a food processor and process until well combined. Scrape into a bowl. Pick the mince up and firmly throw it back into the bowl or onto a clean work surface several times. This removes air pockets and tenderises the meat.

Divide the meat into 8 equal portions. Using wet hands, wrap a ball of mixture around each stalk of lemongrass. (You can make these a day in advance and keep in the fridge.)

Your firepit is ready to cook on after about 2 hours of burning, when the timber is charcoal black, has transformed into red hot coals about the size of golf balls, and the smoke has all but subsided. To test for heat, you should not be able to hold the palm of your hand 5–10 cm (2–4 inches) above the grill for more than 2–3 seconds. Replace the grill over the firepit and give it around 10 minutes to heat up. (See page 9.)

Brush a little oil over the pork and cook on the firepit grill for 10 minutes, turning every minutes until golden and cooked through. Serve with nuoc cham.

SPICY BEEF KEBABS

This recipe uses a simple trick of adding grated onion to the marinade. The acid in the grated onion tenderises the meat in this Moroccan-inspired recipe.

SERVES 4

2 tablespoons grated onion

2 garlic cloves, crushed

2 teaspoons ground cumin

1 teaspoon sweet paprika

1 teaspoon dried chilli flakes

1 handful coriander (cilantro) leaves and stems

1 handful flat-leaf (Italian) parsley leaves and stems

2 tablespoons lemon juice

600 g (1 lb 5 oz) thick cut beef rump steak, cut into chunky 2–3 cm (1 inch) cubes

Lemon wedges, to serve

Put the onion pulp in a small bowl with the garlic, cumin, paprika, chilli flakes, coriander, parsley and lemon juice. Stir to combine.

Put the steak cubes in a non-metallic dish and add the spicy onion mix. Toss together well, so the meat is covered with marinade. Refrigerate for 3–6 hours, stirring the meat from time to time. Remove from the fridge 1 hour before cooking.

Soak 6 bamboo skewers in cold water for 1 hour. Thread 3–4 pieces of meat onto each skewer. Season with sea salt and freshly ground black pepper. Set aside for 30 minutes.

Your firepit is ready to cook on after about 2 hours of burning, when the timber is charcoal black, has transformed into red hot coals about the size of golf balls, and the smoke has all but subsided. To test for heat, you should not be able to hold the palm of your hand 5–10 cm (2–4 inches) above the grill for more than 2–3 seconds. Replace the grill over the firepit and give it around 10 minutes to heat up. (See page 9.)

Put the kebabs on the firepit grill and cook for 15 minutes, turning every few minutes, until brown on all sides. Remove to a serving plate and cover with foil to rest for 5 minutes. Serve with lemon wedges.

SMOKY PORK KEBABS

The pork here is kept quite thick and chunky: larger than you would expect skewered meat to be. But the idea is to slide the tasty and tender medallions of pork off the skewer onto your plate. The paprika gives the pork great colour and a really smoky aroma.

SERVES 4

750 (1 lb 10 oz) pork fillet, cut into 2 cm (¾ in) thick slices

1 teaspoon hot smoked paprika

2 teaspoons sweet paprika

3 garlic cloves, finely chopped

½ cup (125 ml) fino sherry

½ teaspoon dried oregano

Soft baguette or Italian bread rolls, to serve

Put the pork in a non-metallic dish. Stir together the hot and sweet paprika, garlic, sherry and oregano in a small bowl. Pour over the pork and toss to combine well. Cover and refrigerate for 6 hours or overnight.

Remove the pork from the fridge and thread onto 4 metal, or soaked bamboo, skewers. Set aside for 30 minutes.

Your firepit is ready to cook on after about 2 hours of burning, when the timber is charcoal black, has transformed into red hot coals about the size of golf balls, and the smoke has all but subsided. To test for heat, you should not be able to hold the palm of your hand 5–10 cm (2–4 inches) above the grill for more than 2–3 seconds. Replace the grill over the firepit and give it around 10 minutes to heat up. (See page 9.)

Put the skewers on the firepit grill. Cook for 8–10 minutes, turning every 2 minutes or so until golden on all sides. Remove from the heat and allow to rest for 5 minutes. Serve in bread rolls with salad leaves.

LAMB WITH FETA, LEMON AND OREGANO

Lamb loin is prized for its leanness and melt-in-the-mouth tenderness. Because it has little to no fat, cooking time ought to be kept to a minimum. The meat is best appreciated when cooked medium-rare (more on the rare side) and still pink in the centre. These same flavours would work nicely with lamb cutlets or backstrap fillets.

SERVES 4

1 kg (2 lb 4 oz) lamb loin fillets (4–5 fillets)

310 g (11 oz) jar Persian feta in oil

3 tablespoons lemon juice

2 garlic cloves, finely chopped

1 teaspoon dried Greek oregano, plus a little extra, to serve

2 tablespoons finely chopped flat-leaf (Italian) parsley

Lemon wedges, to serve

Put the lamb in a flat non-metallic dish. Mix 1 tablespoon of oil from the jar of feta with the lemon juice, garlic, oregano and parsley. Rub all over the lamb. Cover and set aside for 1 hour.

Your firepit is ready to cook on after about 2 hours of burning, when the timber is charcoal black, has transformed into red hot coals about the size of golf balls, and the smoke has all but subsided. To test for heat, you should not be able to hold the palm of your hand 5–10 cm (2–4 inches) above the grill for more than 2–3 seconds. Replace the grill over the firepit and give it around 10 minutes to heat up. (See page 9.)

Lay the lamb on the firepit grill. Cook for about 10 minutes, simply turning every couple of minutes, until golden all over. These don't need long to cook. Transfer to a plate and rest for 5 minutes. Scatter with the feta and sprinkle with oregano. Serve with lemon wedges.

LAMB WITH BASIL PESTO

Lamb backstrap is used here, which is known as saddle or loin outside Australia and New Zealand. It is pretty much ready to go for cooking on the firepit and needs little more than a rub with olive oil and some salt and pepper. Pesto is used here as a delicious condiment, but chimichurri or baba ghanoush would also work very nicely.

SERVES 4

3 lamb backstrap fillets, about 900 g (2 lb)

1 tablespoon olive oil

1 teaspoon garlic salt

1 teaspoon freshly ground black pepper

Lemon wedges, to serve

BASIL PESTO

2 garlic cloves, chopped

½ teaspoon sea salt

1 bunch flat-leaf (Italian) parsley

1 bunch basil

1 teaspoon dried oregano

100 g (3½ oz) pine nuts, toasted

3 tablespoons olive oil

½ cup (50 g) grated parmesan

3 tablespoons lemon juice

To make the pesto, put the garlic, salt, parsley, basil, oregano and pine nuts in a food processor and pulse to combine into a chunky paste. With the motor running, add the oil until well combined. Transfer to a bowl and stir in the parmesan and some cracked black pepper. Cover and refrigerate (but use on the day it is made). Just before serving, stir in the lemon juice.

Put the lamb in a flat dish. Rub with olive oil. Sprinkle garlic salt and black pepper over both sides of the lamb. Set aside for 30–60 minutes; cover with a clean tea towel if you like.

Your firepit is ready to cook on after about 2 hours of burning, when the timber is charcoal black, has transformed into red hot coals about the size of golf balls, and the smoke has all but subsided. To test for heat, you should not be able to hold the palm of your hand 5–10 cm (2–4 inches) above the grill for more than 2–3 seconds. Replace the grill over the firepit and give it around 10 minutes to heat up. (See page 9.)

Lay the lamb on the firepit grill and cook for 8 minutes, until a golden crust forms. Turn and cook for a further 6 minutes. Transfer to a plate. Cover with foil and rest for 10 minutes.

Slice the lamb and arrange on a serving plate. Spoon pesto over the top and serve with lemon wedges.

VEAL CUTLETS WITH ROSEMARY, ANCHOVIES AND RED WINE

This recipe is a cinch. The flavourings are classic and simple, paying respect to the lovely and very special (they are not the easiest things to find) veal cutlets.

SERVES 4

1 tablespoon rosemary leaves

3 anchovies

3 garlic cloves, chopped

3 tablespoons olive oil

½ cup (125 ml) red wine

4 veal cutlets, 250 g (9 oz) each

Pound the rosemary, anchovies and garlic with a mortar and pestle until the anchovies are mashed. Season well with freshly ground black pepper. Stir through the olive oil and red wine.

Put the cutlets in a non-metallic dish and add the marinade, tossing the cutlets around to coat in the mixture. Cover and refrigerate for 3 hours or overnight, turning often. Remove from the fridge 1 hour before cooking.

Your firepit is ready to cook on after about 2 hours of burning, when the timber is charcoal black, has transformed into red hot coals about the size of golf balls, and the smoke has all but subsided. To test for heat, you should not be able to hold the palm of your hand 5—10 cm (2—4 inches) above the grill for more than 2—3 seconds. Replace the grill over the firepit and give it around 10 minutes to heat up. (See page 9.)

Put the cutlets on the firepit grill and cook for 10 minutes. They should look quite dark from the marinade. If they are cooking too quickly and start to burn, move them to the edge of the firepit where the heat is less intense. Turn and cook for another 5 minutes. Transfer to a tray lined with baking paper. Cover with foil and rest for 10 minutes before serving.

SHEFTALIA

Sheftalia is a traditional Greek and Cypriot grilled meat recipe — lamb mince with a few other simple seasonings thrown in. It's lovely wrapped in warm pitta bread with a bit of tomato salad and some cool yoghurt dressing dolloped in too.

SERVES 4

700 g (1 lb 9 oz) minced (ground) lamb

4 garlic cloves, crushed

2 tablespoons finely chopped flat-leaf (Italian) parsley

2 teaspoons dried Greek oregano, plus a little extra, to serve

1 teaspoon sea salt

4 soft pitta breads, to serve

Put the lamb in a large bowl with the garlic, parsley, oregano, sea salt and some freshly ground black pepper. Use your hands to combine well, throwing the meat against the side of the bowl so it begins to look like a paste.

Lightly wet your hands and divide the meat into 16 equal parts. Roll each into a ball about the size of a golf ball. Put on a tray, cover and refrigerate for 3 hours or overnight.

Thread 4 meatballs onto each of 4 long metal or soaked bamboo skewers. Set aside for 30 minutes.

Your firepit is ready to cook on after about 2 hours of burning, when the timber is charcoal black, has transformed into red hot coals about the size of golf balls, and the smoke has all but subsided. To test for heat, you should not be able to hold the palm of your hand 5–10 cm (2–4 inches) above the grill for more than 2–3 seconds. Replace the grill over the firepit and give it around 10 minutes to heat up. (See page 9.)

Put the skewers on the firepit grill and cook for 15–20 minutes, turning every 5 minutes or so, until cooked through. Serve in warm pitta rolls, with some salad.

LAMB CHOPS WITH ANCHOVY BUTTER

It is not unusual to insert slivers of anchovy and garlic into a leg of lamb before roasting. This gives some culinary kudos to the humble chop. This recipe simplifies it even more by adding anchovies to softened butter which is melted on the grilled lamb. The compound butter also includes tomato which is a fine flavour to pair with both lamb and anchovy.

SERVES 4

12 lamb chops

2 tablespoons olive oil

4 rosemary sprigs

ANCHOVY BUTTER

1 vine-ripened tomato

125 g (4½ oz) unsalted butter, softened

1 garlic clove, crushed

2 anchovies, finely chopped

1 tablespoon finely chopped flat-leaf (Italian) parsley

Make the anchovy butter a day or two in advance. Remove the stem from the tomato and cut out the core. Cut a small shallow cross on the opposite end and place in a small heatproof bowl. Pour enough boiling water over the tomato to cover, then leave in the hot water for 1 minute. Remove and peel away the skin. Cut in half and scoop and discard all the seeds, then cut the flesh into small dice. Mix together the tomato, butter, garlic, anchovies and parsley.

Lay a sheet of plastic wrap on a work surface and spoon the anchovy butter down the centre. Roll the butter in the plastic to make a log, twisting the ends to seal. Refrigerate for up to 2 days, until needed.

Put the lamb chops, olive oil, rosemary and salt and pepper to taste in a dish. Toss well, then cover and leave for 1 hour.

Your firepit is ready to cook on after about 2 hours of burning, when the timber is charcoal black, has transformed into red hot coals about the size of golf balls, and the smoke has all but subsided. To test for heat, you should not be able to hold the palm of your hand 5–10 cm (2–4 inches) above the grill for more than 2–3 seconds. Replace the grill over the firepit and give it around 10 minutes to heat up. (See page 9.)

Put the lamb on the hottest part of the firepit grill and cook for 2–3 minutes on each side, until golden but pink in the centre. Transfer to a plate, cover loosely with foil and rest for 5 minutes. Slice the anchovy butter and serve on the lamb.

ROAST BEEF FILLET WITH PAPRIKA MAYONNAISE

These beef fillets could be made in advance, grilled and just left to sit for a short while before being sliced to serve. Ready when you are. The prosciutto wrapped around the beef is cooked crisp, imparting even more flavour on the tender cut of beef.

SERVES 6–8

1.5 kg (3 lb 5 oz) beef fillet

8 garlic cloves

2 cups (500 ml) Spanish sherry

200 g (7 oz) thinly sliced prosciutto (about 10–12 slices)

8 fresh bay leaves

1 tablespoon olive oil

PAPRIKA MAYONNAISE

¾ cup (185 g) mayonnaise

1 garlic clove, crushed

½ teaspoon smoked paprika

2 teaspoons lemon juice

Trim the beef of any fat and sinew. Cut the garlic into thin slivers. Make incisions all over the beef and slip in the garlic slivers. Lay the beef in a bowl and pour in the sherry. Set aside at room temperature for 2 hours, or cover and refrigerate for several hours or overnight, turning every now and then. Remove from the fridge 1–2 hours before cooking.

Lay the slices of prosciutto, so they overlap slightly, on a work surface.

Remove the beef from the sherry, draining well. Lay the beef on the prosciutto and put the bay leaves on the beef. Wrap the beef and bay leaves up in the prosciutto. Secure with cooking string.

To make the paprika mayonnaise, combine all the ingredients in a small bowl.

Your firepit is ready to cook on after about 2 hours of burning, when the timber is charcoal black, has transformed into red hot coals about the size of golf balls, and the smoke has all but subsided. To test for heat, you should not be able to hold the palm of your hand 5–10 cm (2–4 inches) above the grill for more than 2–3 seconds. Replace the grill over the firepit and give it around 10 minutes to heat up. (See page 9.)

Lay the beef on the firepit grill and cook for 10 minutes each side, until well browned. While the beef is cooking, put a roasting tray on the firepit and allow it to heat up. Pour the olive oil on the tray.

Transfer the beef to the hot tray and cook for 10 minutes each side. Wrap the beef in foil. Return to the edge of the firepit where the heat is less intense, and cook for 15 minutes. Remove the beef and leave wrapped in the foil to rest for 20 minutes. Thickly slice, remove the bay leaves and serve with paprika mayonnaise.

CHINATOWN PORK

You see these unctuous and shiny glazed morsels hanging in Chinatown windows. It's probably a toss-up between roast duck and barbecued pork (char siu) as to which is the most popular. The roast duck is one of those things you would never want to try cooking at home. The pork, on the other hand, is dead easy. All you need are a few Chinatown grocery staples (sauces that will keep for ages in the cupboard) and away you go.

SERVES 4

2 pork fillets, about 400 g (14 oz) each

CHAR SIU GLAZE

1 teaspoon Chinese five-spice powder

2 tablespoons runny honey

2 tablespoons hoisin sauce

2 tablespoons light soy sauce

Put all the glaze ingredients in a non-metallic dish and stir until combined. Add the pork fillets and rub the glaze all over the pork. Cover and refrigerate for 3 hours. Don't marinate it for any longer — the salt content is quite high and, left too long, the meat will become tough and chewy.

Remove from the fridge 30 minutes before cooking.

Your firepit is ready to cook on after about 2 hours of burning, when the timber is charcoal black, has transformed into red hot coals about the size of golf balls, and the smoke has all but subsided. To test for heat, you should not be able to hold the palm of your hand 5—10 cm (2—4 inches) above the grill for more than 2—3 seconds. Replace the grill over the firepit and give it around 10 minutes to heat up. (See page 9.)

Lift the pork out of the marinade, keeping the marinade. Lay the pork on the firepit grill. Cook for 12 minutes, turning every 3 minutes, and brushing every few minutes with the reserved marinade. Lay each fillet on a separate sheet of foil. Brush with any reserved marinade. Wrap the pork in the foil and return to the edge of the firepit grill, where the heat is less intense. Leave for 15 minutes, until the pork is cooked through. Remove and allow to cool to room temperature before slicing onto a serving plate.

RUMP STEAK WITH GINGER, GARLIC AND SOY

Here is my earliest barbecue memory — eating a steak, marinated in these Asian flavours. You can't go past rump steak — if you ask most people what their favourite cut of barbecued steak is, they'll generally say rump. If you are lucky enough to get a really big piece, you will see how it is divided into several muscle groups, separated by lines of fat. The muscle shaped like an elongated tear drop is the most tender.

SERVES 4

2 rump steaks, about 400 g (14 oz) each, about 1.5 cm (⅝ inch) thick

GINGER SOY MARINADE

½ cup (125 ml) light soy sauce, preferably Japanese

1 tablespoon sesame oil

½ teaspoon sugar

2 garlic cloves, roughly chopped

5 cm (2 inch) piece ginger, finely sliced

Mix together the ginger soy marinade ingredients. Put the steak in a large non-metallic dish and add the marinade. Cover and set aside for 1 hour, turning the steak often. You could put the steaks in the fridge for a couple of hours, but no longer: the salt in the soy can make the meat tough. I find the steak has better flavour and texture if left to marinate at room temperature for a shorter time.

Your firepit is ready to cook on after about 2 hours of burning, when the timber is charcoal black, has transformed into red hot coals about the size of golf balls, and the smoke has all but subsided. To test for heat, you should not be able to hold the palm of your hand 5–10 cm (2–4 inches) above the grill for more than 2–3 seconds. Replace the grill over the firepit and give it around 10 minutes to heat up. (See page 9.)

Put the steaks on the firepit grill and cook for 3 minutes on each side. Remove the steaks to a plate, cover lightly with foil and rest for 5 minutes. The steaks will be quite pink in the centre: medium-rare. Cook for 5 minutes each side for medium and 7 minutes each side for well done. Cut each steak in half to serve, or into smaller pieces as part of a barbecue banquet.

MIXED MEAT GRILL

The selection here is merely my suggestion. Use whatever takes your fancy, or looks best at the butcher's. One word of advice, though — you want cuts of meat that don't need a very long cooking time or too much fuss.

SERVES 8 TO SHARE

2 fillet steaks (quite thick — about 3–4 cm/1½ inches), about 150 g (5½ oz) each

2 T-bone steaks, about 150 g (5½ oz) each

8 lamb cutlets

1 garlic bulb, cloves separated, left unpeeled

6 rosemary sprigs

1 small bunch thyme

3 tablespoons olive oil

3 tablespoons sherry vinegar

1 teaspoon freshly ground black pepper

Put the meat in a large roasting tin. Add all the other ingredients and toss everything together so the herbs and garlic are evenly distributed over, under and between the pieces of meat. Cover and refrigerate overnight, tossing a few times.

Remove from the fridge 1 hour before cooking.

Your firepit is ready to cook on after about 2 hours of burning, when the timber is charcoal black, has transformed into red hot coals about the size of golf balls, and the smoke has all but subsided. To test for heat, you should not be able to hold the palm of your hand 5–10 cm (2–4 inches) above the grill for more than 2–3 seconds. Replace the grill over the firepit and give it around 10 minutes to heat up. (See page 9.)

You might need a timer (a smartphone is ideal) or some sort of stopwatch to make things easier here. All the meat is cooked medium-rare.

Put the fillet steaks on the firepit grill and cook for 2 minutes, pressing down occasionally with a flat metal spatula but without moving or turning. When the fillet steaks have been cooking for 2 minutes, add the T-bones. Cook both T-bones and fillet for 4 minutes. Turn both the fillet and T-bones over. Cook for another 4 minutes, then remove the T-bone steaks to a plate and cover with foil. Cook the fillet steaks for another 2 minutes then add to the plate and cover.

Cook the lamb cutlets for 3 minutes on the firepit, then turn and cook for another 2 minutes and add to the other meat. Cover all with foil and leave to rest for 10 minutes.

Serve the mixed grilled meats with an arrangement of sauces and condiments on the side.

LAMB WITH GREEN OLIVE SALSA

Lamb cuts from young animals are perfect for quick cooking — backstrap, fillet, loin chops, cutlets and medallions. But the leg may well be the cut we most associate with lamb. Leaving the skin and fat on helps the meat to cook without burning.

SERVES 6–8

1 small leg of lamb, about 1.6 kg (3 lb 8 oz), butterflied

½ cup (125 ml) dry white wine

3 tablespoons lemon juice

3 tablespoons olive oil, plus extra, for cooking

1 handful rosemary sprigs

10–12 garlic cloves, finely chopped

GREEN OLIVE SALSA

1 cup (175 g) green olives, pitted

6 baby gherkins (cornichons)

2 large handfuls flat-leaf (Italian) parsley

2 large handfuls mint

2 garlic cloves, chopped

3 anchovy fillets

3 tablespoons lemon juice

½ cup (125 ml) olive oil

As the lamb will be thicker at one end, make several deep cuts into that part to allow for even cooking. Put the lamb in a large non-metallic dish with the wine, lemon juice, olive oil, rosemary and garlic. Set aside at room temperature for 2–3 hours or cover and refrigerate for up to a day, turning often. Remove from the fridge 1 hour before cooking.

To make the green olive salsa, put all the ingredients in a food processor and mix to a paste.

Your firepit is ready to cook on after about 2 hours of burning, when the timber is charcoal black, has transformed into red hot coals about the size of golf balls, and the smoke has all but subsided. To test for heat, you should not be able to hold the palm of your hand 5–10 cm (2–4 inches) above the grill for more than 2–3 seconds. Replace the grill over the firepit and give it around 10 minutes to heat up. (See page 9.)

Lay the lamb on the firepit grill and cook for 15 minutes. Move the lamb around if it is starting to burn. Turn the lamb over and cook for a further 15 minutes. Wrap in foil and put on the edge of the firepit where the heat is less intense. Cook for a further 15 minutes.

Remove the lamb, but leave wrapped in the foil to rest for 20 minutes before serving. Serve thickly sliced, with the green olive salsa spooned over the top.

BUTTERFLIED LAMB MASALA

Do keep your eye on this one. It is thick in parts so it is not to be rushed, causing it to burn before cooking on the inside. Having said this, lamb is best pink. But if that is not your thing, cook on low heat for an extra 15 or 20 minutes. And let it sit, covered, at the edge of the firepit for 20 minutes. The green masala marinade is a base paste that can be also be used for curries. Just fry in a little oil, add some cubed lamb or beef, top with water and cook over very low heat until the meat is fork tender.

SERVES 8

1 small leg lamb, about 1.8 kg (4 lb), butterflied

GREEN MASALA MARINADE

1 tablespoon black mustard seeds

1 tablespoon cumin seeds

1 tablespoon coriander seeds

1 teaspoon turmeric

4 cardamom pods

1 cinnamon stick, broken up

4 spring onions (scallions), finely chopped

4 garlic cloves

3 large green chillies

1 small bunch coriander (cilantro), chopped

1 tablespoon finely grated ginger

½ teaspoon freshly ground black pepper

3 tablespoons olive oil

3 tablespoons lemon juice

For the green masala marinade, put the mustard seeds, cumin seeds, coriander seeds, turmeric, cardamom and cinnamon in a small dry frying pan over high heat. Shake the pan until the mustard seeds pop and the mixture gives off an aromatic smoke. Allow to cool then grind in a small spice mill (or mortar and pestle) to a rough powder.

Put the ground spices in a food processor with the other marinade ingredients and whiz to a chunky darkish-green paste. Remove to a bowl. This can be made in advance and kept in a non-metallic dish, covered, in the fridge.

Cut 5 mm (¼ inch) deep incisions on the skin side of the lamb, about 5 cm (2 inches) apart. This will help the lamb to cook more evenly and allow the intense flavour of the marinade to penetrate the meat.

Put the lamb in a large, flat non-metallic dish with the masala marinade. Rub in the marinade, getting it into the cuts you have made. Cover and refrigerate overnight, turning once during this time. Remove from the fridge at least 1 hour before cooking.

Your firepit is ready to cook on after about 2 hours of burning, when the timber is charcoal black, has transformed into red hot coals about the size of golf balls, and the smoke has all but subsided. To test for heat, you should not be able to hold the palm of your hand 5–10 cm (2–4 inches) above the grill for more than 2–3 seconds. Replace the grill over the firepit and give it around 10 minutes to heat up. (See page 9.)

Lay the lamb on the firepit grill and cook for 15 minutes. Move the lamb around if starting to burn. Turn the lamb and cook for a further 15 minutes. Wrap in foil and put on the edge of the firepit where the heat is less intense. Cook for a further 15 minutes. Move the lamb, leaving wrapped in foil to rest for 20 minutes before serving.

BEEF RIB-EYE WITH HORSERADISH BUTTER

This is a good example of how meat can benefit from sitting at room temperature before cooking, and from resting after cooking. Rib-eye does not require much cooking — this means that if you cook it straight from the fridge it will still be cold in the middle. It doesn't generally have much fat, so, if overcooked it will be dry and if not rested it will be tough. Basically, this cut deserves a little respect.

SERVES 4

800 g (1 lb 12 oz) beef rib-eye fillet

1 teaspoon sea salt

1 teaspoon freshly ground black pepper

1 tablespoon olive oil

HORSERADISH BUTTER

125 g (4½ oz) unsalted butter, softened to room temperature

1 tablespoon finely grated fresh horseradish

2 teaspoons Worcestershire sauce

1 garlic clove, crushed

1 tablespoon finely chopped spring onion (scallion)

1 tablespoon small salted capers, rinsed

2 anchovies

2 tablespoons finely chopped flat-leaf (Italian) parsley

To make the horseradish butter, put all the ingredients in a food processor and mix well. Lay a sheet of plastic wrap on a work surface. Put spoonfuls of the butter along the centre of the plastic, then firmly wrap and form into a log about 2 cm (¾ in) wide. Refrigerate for 2–3 hours, or until firm.

Rub the beef all over with the salt and pepper and set aside at room temperature for 1–2 hours.

Your firepit is ready to cook on after about 2 hours of burning, when the timber is charcoal black, has transformed into red hot coals about the size of golf balls, and the smoke has all but subsided. To test for heat, you should not be able to hold the palm of your hand 5–10 cm (2–4 inches) above the grill for more than 2–3 seconds. Replace the grill over the firepit and give it around 10 minutes to heat up. (See page 9.)

Put a baking tray on the firepit grill. Leave for 10 minutes to heat up. Drizzle the olive oil over the tray. Put the beef on the tray and cook for 20 minutes, turning every 5 minutes, so each side is well browned.

Wrap the beef in foil, ensuring the foil is firmly sealed. Put on the edge of the firepit and cook for 15 minutes. Remove and leave to rest for 15 minutes, wrapped in the foil.

Thickly slice and serve with slices of the butter on top.

NEW YORK COWBOY

A New York cut steak is also called porterhouse. It is a thick cut of beef, about 2–3 cm (1 inch), with a healthy layer of fat hugging one side. Like most people, I sometimes use the internet when I'm doing research. While I was looking at recipes I found a spice rub called New York cowboy spice rub. Intrigued? I was; especially when I saw that it asked for 6 tablespoons of salt in the mixture! Mental note, don't automatically assume the written word on the internet is gospel. If I had followed this I would have ruined some expensive meat. But, I do like the name of the rub, so here is my version.

SERVES 4

4 New York or sirloin steaks, about 200 g (7 oz) each

1 tablespoon olive oil

2 red onions, finely sliced

2 teaspoons sea salt flakes

NEW YORK COWBOY SPICE RUB

2 teaspoons chilli powder

2 teaspoons sweet paprika

2 teaspoons black peppercorns

4 garlic cloves, crushed

4 tablespoons olive oil

To make the spice rub, put the chilli powder, paprika and black peppercorns in a spice mill and whiz together until the peppercorns are crushed and the mixture is powder-like.

Put the powder in a large non-metallic dish, add the garlic and oil and stir to make a fiery red paste. Add the steaks and rub the paste all over them.

Cover and refrigerate for 6 hours or overnight. Remove from the fridge 1 hour before cooking. These are thick cuts of meat so they will need to come to room temperature, otherwise the steaks will still be fridge cold in the centre when you eat them.

Your firepit is ready to cook on after about 2 hours of burning, when the timber is charcoal black, has transformed into red hot coals about the size of golf balls, and the smoke has all but subsided. To test for heat, you should not be able to hold the palm of your hand 5–10 cm (2–4 inches) above the grill for more than 2–3 seconds. Replace the grill over the firepit and give it around 10 minutes to heat up. (See page 9.)

Put a baking tray on the firepit grill and leave for 10 minutes to heat up. Pour the oil onto the tray and scatter with the sliced onions. Stir the onions and cook for 8–10 minutes, until charred. Remove the tray from the grill.

Sprinkle the salt on the steaks, put on the firepit grill and cook for 6 minutes. Turn over and cook for another 6 minutes. Wrap the meat in foil and sit the steaks on the edge of the firepit for 5 minutes. Serve with charred onions scattered over the top.

CHAR SIU LAMB WRAPS

You might not associate cumin with Chinese flavours; however, in the north and west of China, lamb and wheat is abundant and dominates the cooking. So in that area you find lots of barbecued lamb flavoured with chilli and cumin and served with steamed buns and breads. Very nice.

SERVES 4

2 large lamb backstrap fillets, about 400 g (14 oz) each

2 teaspoons sesame oil

2 garlic cloves, finely chopped

2 teaspoons dried chilli flakes

2 teaspoons ground cumin

3 tablespoons Chinese barbecue sauce (char siu), plus extra, for serving

4 soft tortillas or burritos

4 spring onions (scallions), thinly sliced

2 Lebanese cucumbers, sliced

Put the lamb in a bowl with the sesame oil, garlic, chilli and cumin. Toss the lamb around to coat all over with the marinade. Cover and set aside at room temperature for a couple of hours or cover and refrigerate for 3–6 hours. Remove from the fridge 1 hour before cooking.

Your firepit is ready to cook on after about 2 hours of burning, when the timber is charcoal black, has transformed into red hot coals about the size of golf balls, and the smoke has all but subsided. To test for heat, you should not be able to hold the palm of your hand 5–10 cm (2–4 inches) above the grill for more than 2–3 seconds. Replace the grill over the firepit and give it around 10 minutes to heat up. (See page 9.)

Put the lamb on the firepit grill and cook for 2 minutes. Turn over and cook for another 2 minutes. Brush the lamb with the barbecue sauce and turn. Continue to baste and turn the lamb, using all the remaining sauce for 4–5 minutes. Remove the lamb to a chopping board and cover loosely with foil for 5 minutes.

Slice the lamb. Spread a little barbecue sauce down the centre of each tortilla. Top with sliced lamb, spring onions and cucumbers. Roll up to serve.

PARCHMENT BAKED WHITING WITH LEMON SALSA BUTTER 112

WHOLE BABY TROUT WITH LEMON AND DILL 115

LAKSA PRAWN SKEWERS 116

SWORDFISH KEBABS 119

SEAFOOD LEMONGRASS SKEWERS 120

FIREPIT WHITING 123

BARBECUED SNAPPER WITH MEXICAN SALSA 124

SAGANAKI PRAWNS 127

PRAWN AND CHORIZO SKEWERS 128

LOBSTER TAILS WITH CHILLI AND GARLIC BUTTER 131

SICILIAN FISH 132

FIVE-SPICE FISH PARCELS 135

WHOLE SNAPPER WITH GINGER AND SPRING ONIONS 136

WHOLE FISH WITH JALAPEÑO CHILLIES, LEMON AND HERBS 139

OCEAN TROUT FILLET WITH GINGER AND SHALLOTS 140

NEWSPAPER-WRAPPED SALMON WITH FRESH HERBS, LEMON AND CHILLI 143

SEAFOOD

PARCHMENT BAKED WHITING WITH LEMON SALSA BUTTER

It seems very 1970s to wrap something — usually white fish fillets — in paper and cook in the oven. But it's a cleverly delicate method to cook a rather delicate fish — and it translates well to the firepit. I've made it more contemporary by throwing in some green chilli and coriander. I use whiting here, but any firm white fish will do.

SERVES 4

2 whiting fillets, about 375 g (13 oz) each

LEMON SALSA BUTTER

125 g (4½ oz) butter

1 large handful coriander (cilantro), finely chopped

3 spring onions (scallions), finely chopped

1 tablespoon finely snipped chives

1 large green chilli, seeded and finely chopped

2 tablespoons lemon juice

To make the lemon salsa butter, put the butter in a small saucepan and gently melt over low heat. Add the other lemon salsa ingredients, with a pinch of sea salt and some freshly ground black pepper. Stir for a minute or so to combine, then set aside to cool to room temperature.

Tear off 2 pieces of baking paper, large enough with room to spare to wrap a whiting fillet in. Sit a fillet in the centre of the paper and spoon over half the salsa butter. Bring the 2 long sides of the paper together and firmly fold over a few times, then twist the ends to seal. Tie each twisted end with kitchen string. Now sit the parcel on a large piece of foil. Fold the edges of the foil to firmly seal and form a parcel. Repeat with the other whiting fillet.

Your firepit is ready to cook on after about 2 hours of burning, when the timber is charcoal black, has transformed into red hot coals about the size of golf balls, and the smoke has all but subsided. To test for heat, you should not be able to hold the palm of your hand 5–10 cm (2–4 inches) above the grill for more than 2–3 seconds. Replace the grill over the firepit and give it around 10 minutes to heat up. (See page 9.)

Put the fish parcels on the firepit grill and cook for 10 minutes. The fish will be white and flaky and can be served directly from the parcel.

WHOLE BABY TROUT WITH LEMON AND DILL

The trick here is to cook the fish (as I do with much seafood cooked over an open flame) on a couple of sheets of baking paper directly placed on the grill. It prevents the delicate skin from sticking and makes it easy to move the fish around on the firepit without breaking it up.

SERVES 4

2 trout, each about 500 g
(1 lb 2 oz), cleaned and gutted

1 lemon, very finely sliced

1 red onion, very finely sliced

1 bunch dill

Olive oil, for brushing

Lay the trout on a clean work surface. Inside the cavity of each trout put 3–4 slices of lemon, a few slices of red onion, 3–4 sprigs of dill, then another layer of onion and lemon. Season the outside of the fish well with sea salt and freshly ground black pepper.

Your firepit is ready to cook on after about 2 hours of burning, when the timber is charcoal black, has transformed into red hot coals about the size of golf balls, and the smoke has all but subsided. To test for heat, you should not be able to hold the palm of your hand 5–10 cm (2–4 inches) above the grill for more than 2–3 seconds. Replace the grill over the firepit and give it around 10 minutes to heat up. (See page 9.)

Tear off 2 sheets of baking paper about 30 cm (12 inches) square. Lightly brush the paper with olive oil. Put the remaining dill on the paper and lay the fish on top of the dill.

Use the edges of the paper to lift and transfer the fish onto the firepit grill. Cook for 10 minutes, then turn over and cook for another 8–10 minutes, until the flesh of the fish easily pulls away from the bones. One fish can be shared between two people.

LAKSA PRAWN SKEWERS

Some say the word laksa means 'ten thousand', which refers to the number of ingredients needed to make an authentic paste. Good-quality ready-made pastes are available and they are used in coconut milk-based soups, with thin rice noodles, chicken, fried tofu and bean sprouts, with some fresh lime on the side to cut through the richness. The paste, made creamy with a little coconut milk and balanced with sugar and salty fish sauce, also makes a great easy marinade for big prawns and would work well as a marinade for chicken.

SERVES 4

½ cup (125 ml) coconut cream

2 tablespoons good-quality laksa paste

1 tablespoon fish sauce

1 tablespoon brown sugar

½ cup (125 ml) coconut milk

3 limes, cut into quarters

24 large raw prawns (shrimp), deveined

Put the coconut cream in a small saucepan and bring to the boil for about 5 minutes, until little volcanic-like pools form, bubbling as the oil separates from the liquid. Stir as the coconut cream darkens around the edge and boil for another 2 minutes until it looks curdled.

Stir in the laksa paste, add the fish sauce and sugar and cook for 1 minute. The mixture will look dark at this stage. Stir in the coconut milk and bring to the boil for 1 minute. Leave to cool completely.

Put the prawns in a non-metallic dish, pour in the laksa marinade and toss to coat the prawns evenly. Cover and refrigerate for 3 hours. Soak 12 bamboo skewers in cold water for an hour.

Reserving the marinade, thread 2 prawns onto each skewer with a lime wedge on the end.

Your firepit is ready to cook on after about 2 hours of burning, when the timber is charcoal black, has transformed into red hot coals about the size of golf balls, and the smoke has all but subsided. To test for heat, you should not be able to hold the palm of your hand 5–10 cm (2–4 inches) above the grill for more than 2–3 seconds. Replace the grill over the firepit and give it around 10 minutes to heat up. (See page 9.)

Put the skewers on the firepit grill and cook for 2–3 minutes. Turn over and cook for another couple of minutes, until the prawns are pink all over. Start brushing the prawns with the reserved marinade, turn and cook for 1 minute. Repeat once more — the prawns should be golden as the paste is cooked onto the shell. Serve with finger bowls and bowls for shells.

SWORDFISH KEBABS

Great swordfish, to me, is about the texture of the meat. And this is a meaty fish. Like tuna, it lends itself to being cooked as you would a steak. It is an ideal fish to cook on the firepit as it's firm enough to hold its form.

SERVES 4

750 g (1 lb 10 oz) swordfish steaks, skin removed, cut into 3–4 cm (1½ inch) pieces

3 tablespoons olive oil

4 garlic cloves, finely chopped

3 tablespoons finely chopped flat-leaf (Italian) parsley

3 tablespoons lemon juice

4 roma (plum) tomatoes, quartered

2 red onions, cut into wedges

1 green capsicum (pepper), cut into 2 cm (¾ inch) pieces

2 lemons, cut into cheeks

Put the swordfish in a non-metallic bowl with the olive oil, garlic, parsley and lemon juice. Leave at room temperature for 30 minutes.

Reserving the marinade, thread pieces of fish, tomato, onion and capsicum onto 8 long metal skewers.

Your firepit is ready to cook on after about 2 hours of burning, when the timber is charcoal black, has transformed into red hot coals about the size of golf balls, and the smoke has all but subsided. To test for heat, you should not be able to hold the palm of your hand 5–10 cm (2–4 inches) above the grill for more than 2–3 seconds. Replace the grill over the firepit and give it around 10 minutes to heat up. (See page 9.)

Put the lemon cheeks, cut side down, on the firepit grill and cook for 5–10 minutes, until charred. Transfer to a plate.

Lay the skewers on the grill and cook for about 10 minutes, turning every 2 minutes and basting with the reserved marinade, until the fish is cooked through. Sprinkle with a generous amount of sea salt and some ground black pepper. Serve with the chargrilled lemon cheeks to squeeze over.

SEAFOOD LEMONGRASS SKEWERS

This recipe has Vietnam written all over it. Simple, fresh flavours, with the characteristic lemongrass, of course, which I use here as a skewer. Tinned sugarcane, split or cut into thinner pieces, also works as an effective and exotic skewer.

SERVES 6

5 large red chillies, chopped

4 garlic cloves, chopped

4 spring onions (scallions), chopped

¼ teaspoon ground turmeric

½ teaspoon ground coriander

1 teaspoon shrimp paste

2 tablespoons tamarind purée

2 makrut lime leaves, finely shredded

1 tablespoon finely chopped lemongrass, white part only

2 tablespoons vegetable oil, plus a little extra, for brushing

3 tablespoons coconut cream

2 tablespoons brown sugar

400 g (14 oz) raw prawn (shrimp) meat

400 g (14 oz) white fish fillet

6 lemongrass stalks, cut into 15 cm (6 inch) lengths, to make 12 skewers

Coriander (cilantro), to serve

Put the chilli, garlic, spring onions, turmeric, ground coriander, shrimp paste, tamarind purée, lime leaves, chopped lemongrass, oil, coconut cream and brown sugar in a food processor. Mix until finely chopped and scrape into a bowl.

Put the prawn meat and fish in the food processor and process to a mince. Scrape into the bowl with the spice mix and stir well.

With wet hands, take 3 heaped tablespoons of the mixture and form a log around each skewer of lemongrass.

Your firepit is ready to cook on after about 2 hours of burning, when the timber is charcoal black, has transformed into red hot coals about the size of golf balls, and the smoke has all but subsided. To test for heat, you should not be able to hold the palm of your hand 5—10 cm (2—4 inches) above the grill for more than 2—3 seconds. Replace the grill over the firepit and give it around 10 minutes to heat up. (See page 9.)

Brush the seafood with the extra oil. Lay on the firepit grill and cook for 5 minutes. Carefully turn over and cook for another 5 minutes. Serve sprinkled with coriander.

FIREPIT WHITING

Whether we cook for a living, cook for a family or only cook on the weekend, it is easy to forget the simple things. And this always strikes me as a little odd when it is the simple things that are often the most important. Cooking doesn't get much simpler (or more impressive) than this. It's the type of dish that fond food memories are made of.

SERVES 4

2 whole whiting, about 450–500 g (1 lb) each, cleaned and gutted

2 tablespoons olive oil

2 teaspoons sea salt

Lemon wedges, to serve

Make a couple of slashes in each side of the fish. Put the fish on a plate and lightly brush each side with olive oil.

Your firepit is ready to cook on after about 2 hours of burning, when the timber is charcoal black, has transformed into red hot coals about the size of golf balls, and the smoke has all but subsided. To test for heat, you should not be able to hold the palm of your hand 5–10 cm (2–4 inches) above the grill for more than 2–3 seconds. Replace the grill over the firepit and give it around 10 minutes to heat up. (See page 9.)

Put a large non-stick frying pan on the firepit grill. Give it 10 minutes or so to heat up.

Drizzle the remaining olive oil into the pan, then sprinkle with salt. Lay the fish in the pan and cook for 5 minutes, without moving so it develops an even, golden crust. Use a large spatula to turn the fish and cook for another 3–4 minutes without moving. The skin should be slightly crispy and the flesh firm yet succulent. Serve with lemon wedges.

BARBECUED SNAPPER WITH MEXICAN SALSA

The same smoky flavour you get when cooking eggplant (aubergine) for baba ghanoush can be achieved with any other soft vegies, such as tomatoes, garlic and shallots. If you decide to go down the Thai flavour path, these vegies would be peeled and processed with some fish sauce and sugar. Or you could take a completely different turn and add some Mexican flavours, such as fiery chipotle and coriander, as I've done here.

SERVES 6

1 large snapper, about 2 kg (4 lb 8 oz), cleaned, gutted and scaled

2 tablespoons olive oil, plus extra, for cooking

2 teaspoons sea salt

Coriander (cilantro), roughly chopped, to serve

Lime wedges, to serve

MEXICAN SALSA

2 tomatoes

1 onion, skin left on and halved

2 garlic cloves, chopped

3 tablespoons freshly squeezed orange juice

2 tablespoons red wine vinegar

1 tablespoon chipotle chilli powder

2 tablespoons brown sugar

1 small bunch coriander (cilantro), roughly chopped

Your firepit is ready to cook on after about 2 hours of burning, when the timber is charcoal black, has transformed into red hot coals about the size of golf balls, and the smoke has all but subsided. To test for heat, you should not be able to hold the palm of your hand 5–10 cm (2–4 inches) above the grill for more than 2–3 seconds. Replace the grill over the firepit and give it around 10 minutes to heat up. (See page 9.)

To make the Mexican salsa, put the tomatoes and onion on the firepit grill, turning constantly and removing when the skin is charred and blistered. Allow to cool.

Peel the vegetables, roughly chop and put in a food processor with the garlic, orange juice, vinegar, chipotle chilli powder, brown sugar and coriander. Process to a smooth paste.

Make a parcel for the fish. Tear off a large sheet of foil that is both longer and wider than the fish. Tear off a similar-sized sheet of baking paper and lay on top of the foil. Make several deep, diagonal cuts across each side of the fish. Combine the olive oil and sea salt in a bowl and rub all over the fish, getting it into the cuts.

Lay the fish on the baking paper and rub the salsa onto each side of the fish. Cover the fish with another sheet of baking paper, then foil. Fold over the sides to make a parcel.

Put a baking tray on the firepit grill and allow to heat up for around 10 minutes. Put the fish on the baking tray and cook for 25–30 minutes, until the flesh easily pulls away from the bones. Lift the parcel onto a chopping board. Serve directly from the parcel.

SAGANAKI PRAWNS

In Greek cooking, saganaki refers to cheese cooked in individual dishes or pans and this dish is popular at tavernas, bistros and tapas joints, served with bread. The prawns here are an addition. I cooked this in one large frying pan; but it is understandable if you don't want to muck up one of your good frying pans from the kitchen on the firepit. I use a couple of frying pans I picked up at my local second-hand charity store especially for cooking on the firepit.

SERVES 4–6

4 tablespoons olive oil

1 red onion, thinly sliced

6 garlic cloves, chopped

1 teaspoon dried Greek oregano

4 tablespoons ouzo

2 x 400 g (14 oz) tins crushed tomatoes

3 tablespoons tomato paste

24 large, raw prawns (shrimp), peeled and deveined

250 g (9 oz) Greek feta, crumbled

1 handful chopped flat-leaf (Italian) parsley, to serve

Lemon wedges, to serve

Heat the olive oil in a saucepan over medium heat. Add the onion, garlic and oregano. Cook for 4–5 minutes, until the onion has softened. Increase the heat to high. Add the ouzo, allowing it to sizzle. When the ouzo has reduced by about half, stir in the tomatoes and tomato paste. Season with salt and pepper to taste. Bring to the boil and cook for just 2–3 minutes. Remove from the heat. (This can be made in advance and kept in the fridge for 2–3 days.)

Your firepit is ready to cook on after about 2 hours of burning, when the timber is charcoal black, has transformed into red hot coals about the size of golf balls, and the smoke has all but subsided. To test for heat, you should not be able to hold the palm of your hand 5–10 cm (2–4 inches) above the grill for more than 2–3 seconds. Replace the grill over the firepit and give it around 10 minutes to heat up. (See page 9.)

Put a large cast-iron skillet or ovenproof frying pan on the firepit grill. Give it 10 minutes or so to heat up. Pour the sauce into the frying pan. You want it to be bubbling hot before adding the prawns. Arrange the prawns in the sauce, leaving a bit of space between them. Cook for 5–8 minutes, until pink and just cooked through.

Crumble the feta into the pan and cook for another minute. Scatter with parsley and serve with lemon wedges.

PRAWN AND CHORIZO SKEWERS

Raw chorizo is used here, so it needs to be cooked before eating. Chorizo should be a deep, rich colour and jam-packed with garlic and paprika. Please don't use the chorizo that looks like cabanossi.

SERVES 4

3 raw chorizo, about 350 g (12 oz)

16 large raw prawns (shrimp), peeled and deveined, leaving the tails intact

2 tablespoons olive oil

2 tablespoons lemon juice

½ teaspoon good-quality dried mint

Lemon cheeks, to serve

Cut each chorizo into chunks similar in thickness to the prawns. Put the chorizo in a bowl with the prawns, olive oil, lemon juice and mint. Toss well. Leave at room temperature for 30 minutes or cover and refrigerate for 3–6 hours. Remove from the fridge 30 minutes before cooking.

Keeping the marinade, thread the chorizo and prawns onto 4 long metal skewers.

Your firepit is ready to cook on after about 2 hours of burning, when the timber is charcoal black, has transformed into red hot coals about the size of golf balls, and the smoke has all but subsided. To test for heat, you should not be able to hold the palm of your hand 5–10 cm (2–4 inches) above the grill for more than 2–3 seconds. Replace the grill over the firepit and give it around 10 minutes to heat up. (See page 9.)

Lay the skewers on the firepit grill and cook for 4–5 minutes on each side, or until cooked through. Brush with the reserved marinade and cook for another minute on each side. Serve with the lemon cheeks.

LOBSTER TAILS WITH CHILLI AND GARLIC BUTTER

There is something about the expense of lobster that puts pressure on the cook to do something really fancy with it. And that is where mistakes are made! No béchamel or white sauce; no cheese and no flambé, please. Keep it simple. Cook the lobster simply and quickly, basting with some lovely, fresh flavours. That's all you need to do. These are made for firepit cooking.

SERVES 4

2 lobster tails, about 320 g (11 oz) each

75 g (2½ oz) unsalted butter, softened to room temperature

½ teaspoon dried chilli flakes

2 garlic cloves, crushed

1 tablespoon finely chopped flat-leaf (Italian) parsley

Lemon wedges, to serve

Cut the lobster tails in half lengthways. Mix together the butter, chilli flakes, garlic and parsley and spread over the cut sides of the lobster.

Your firepit is ready to cook on after about 2 hours of burning, when the timber is charcoal black, has transformed into red hot coals about the size of golf balls, and the smoke has all but subsided. To test for heat, you should not be able to hold the palm of your hand 5–10 cm (2–4 inches) above the grill for more than 2–3 seconds. Replace the grill over the firepit and give it around 10 minutes to heat up. (See page 9.)

Lay the lobster, shell side down, on the firepit grill. The shell will act as a cooking vessel of sorts. Cook for 10–15 minutes, until the lobster meat is white and cooked through. It should peel away easily from the shell. If necessary, cook for a few extra minutes until it does so. Serve with lemon wedges.

SICILIAN FISH

The bright and sunny flavours of Sicily are evident here. Chilli, fennel and lemon combine to make a simple baste, which is rubbed into the fish. This one takes very little time and effort to throw together. Staples such as dried chilli flakes and fennel seeds have a long shelf life and are great to keep in the pantry for any seafood, chicken and pork dishes.

SERVES 6

1 big snapper, about 2 kg (4 lb 8 oz), cleaned, gutted and scaled

1 teaspoon dried chilli flakes

1 teaspoon fennel seeds

2 garlic cloves, chopped

1 teaspoon sea salt

3 tablespoons olive oil

2 lemons, thinly sliced

Make several, deep diagonal cuts on both sides of the fish.

Mix together the chilli flakes, fennel seeds, garlic, sea salt and olive oil in a small bowl.

Tear off a sheet of foil, ensuring it is larger than the fish. Tear off a similar sized sheet of baking paper and lay this on top of the foil. Put the fish on the baking paper. Rub the chilli oil mixture all over the fish and into the cuts. Scatter the lemon slices over the fish.

Lay another sheet of baking paper and then foil over the fish. Fold up the edges to seal. Set aside for 20 minutes.

Your firepit is ready to cook on after about 2 hours of burning, when the timber is charcoal black, has transformed into red hot coals about the size of golf balls, and the smoke has all but subsided. To test for heat, you should not be able to hold the palm of your hand 5–10 cm (2–4 inches) above the grill for more than 2–3 seconds. Replace the grill over the firepit and give it around 10 minutes to heat up. (See page 9.)

Lay the fish on the firepit grill and cook for 35–40 minutes. Remove from the heat but leave wrapped in the parcel for 10 minutes. Serve with lemon wedges.

FIVE-SPICE FISH PARCELS

Okay, so eagle-eyed cooks will see there are only four spices here. Sichuan pepper would also be included in any traditional five-spice mixture, which is so beloved in Chinese cookery. (Although, there is also a Bengali five-spice combination called panch phora — but that's another thing altogether.)

SERVES 4

4 blue-eye trevalla fillets, or any firm white-fleshed fish, around 200 g (7 oz) each

FIVE-SPICE SAUCE

8 star anise

4 whole cloves

½ teaspoon fennel seeds

4 small cinnamon sticks

3 tablespoons light soy sauce

1 tablespoon shaved palm sugar (jaggery) or dark brown sugar

1 tablespoon finely grated ginger

Combine all the sauce ingredients in a small saucepan. Bring to the boil over high heat, stirring to dissolve the sugar. Reduce the heat and simmer for 2–3 minutes. Pour into a large bowl and leave to cool.

Add the fish to the sauce, tossing to coat all over. Cover and refrigerate for up to 3 hours. Remove from the fridge 30 minutes before cooking.

Tear off 4 sheets of baking paper large enough to wrap a piece of the fish entirely. Wet the paper, then shake off any excess water.

Sit a piece of fish in the centre of each piece of paper. Spoon on the sauce, ensuring you have 2 star anise, 1 whole clove and 1 cinnamon stick on each fish fillet. Wrap the fish in the paper to firmly enclose.

Your firepit is ready to cook on after about 2 hours of burning, when the timber is charcoal black, has transformed into red hot coals about the size of golf balls, and the smoke has all but subsided. To test for heat, you should not be able to hold the palm of your hand 5–10 cm (2–4 inches) above the grill for more than 2–3 seconds. Replace the grill over the firepit and give it around 10 minutes to heat up. (See page 9.)

Sit the parcels on the firepit grill and cook for 10 minutes. Move to the edge of the firepit and leave for 5 minutes to rest before serving.

WHOLE SNAPPER WITH GINGER AND SPRING ONIONS

This is a classic Chinese dish, usually all done in a restaurant kitchen. But it is all smoke and mirrors — all you are really doing is assembling. The celestial duo of spring onions and ginger has heavenly status in Chinese cooking, so honour them and only use the freshest. Again, a few simple barbecuing tricks here are the only prerequisites for a perfectly steamed fish.

SERVES 4—5

1 large, whole snapper, about 2 kg (4 lb 8 oz), cleaned and gutted

3 tablespoons Chinese rice wine

10 cm (4 inch) piece of ginger

1 bunch spring onions (scallions)

1 bunch coriander (cilantro), chopped

3 tablespoons light soy sauce

3 tablespoons chicken stock

1 teaspoon sugar

3 tablespoons vegetable oil

1 tablespoon sesame oil

½ teaspoon white pepper

Cut several diagonal incisions across the skin and flesh of the fish. Put the fish in a large non-metallic dish and pour the rice wine over it. Cut the piece of ginger in half and cut one half into thin discs. Cut half the spring onions into 10 cm (4 inch) lengths. Put the ginger discs, spring onion pieces and half the coriander in the cavity of the fish. Cover and set aside for 20 minutes.

Peel and cut the remaining ginger into thin matchsticks. Cut the remaining spring onions into similar-sized pieces to the ginger.

Combine the soy, chicken stock and sugar in a small bowl, stir to dissolve the sugar.

Tear off a sheet of foil, ensuring it is larger than the fish. Tear off a similar-sized sheet of baking paper and lay this on the foil. Put the fish on the baking paper. Now lay another sheet of baking paper and then foil over the fish. Fold around the edges to seal. Set aside for 20 minutes.

Your firepit is ready to cook on after about 2 hours of burning, when the timber is charcoal black, has transformed into red hot coals about the size of golf balls, and the smoke has all but subsided. To test for heat, you should not be able to hold the palm of your hand 5—10 cm (2—4 inches) above the grill for more than 2—3 seconds. Replace the grill over the firepit and give it around 10 minutes to heat up. (See page 9.)

Put the fish parcel on the firepit grill and cook for 30 minutes. Leaving the fish wrapped, transfer to a serving platter. Unwrap the parcel and pour the sauce over the fish. Scatter with the ginger and spring onions.

Put the vegetable oil and sesame oil in a small frying pan and place on the firepit. When the oil is smoking hot, pour it over the fish then quickly scatter with the remaining coriander and white pepper to serve.

WHOLE FISH WITH JALAPEÑO CHILLIES, LEMON AND HERBS

Cooking fish in foil or baking paper is not a new idea. One of the most simple yet tasty recipes is to wrap fish fillets in baking paper with nothing more than lemon slices, dill and butter. This recipe has more of a punch with the inclusion of jalapeños.

SERVES 4

4 small, whole, white-fleshed fish, such as snapper, about 400 g (14 oz) each, cleaned, gutted and scaled

1 lemon, thinly sliced

100 g (3½ oz) unsalted butter, diced

2 tablespoons chopped dill

1 tablespoon finely chopped flat-leaf (Italian) parsley

2 tablespoons finely chopped jalapeño chillies in brine, drained

3 tablespoons lemon juice

Rinse the fish with cold water and pat dry. Tear off 4 large pieces of foil and place 4 slightly smaller pieces of baking paper on top. Put a fish on each.

Put some lemon slices inside the cavity of each fish. Put about 1 tablespoon of butter on top of each fish, top with the herbs and chilli and pour over the lemon juice. Season well with sea salt and freshly ground black pepper. Cover with the cooking foil and fold over the edges to make a parcel.

Your firepit is ready to cook on after about 2 hours of burning, when the timber is charcoal black, has transformed into red hot coals about the size of golf balls, and the smoke has all but subsided. To test for heat, you should not be able to hold the palm of your hand 5–10 cm (2–4 inches) above the grill for more than 2–3 seconds. Replace the grill over the firepit and give it around 10 minutes to heat up. (See page 9.)

Put the fish parcels on the firepit grill and cook for 10 minutes. Remove and leave wrapped in the foil for 5 minutes before opening the parcels to serve.

OCEAN TROUT FILLET WITH GINGER AND SHALLOTS

Ocean trout is a terrifically coloured fish. Beautiful to look at and beautiful to eat. Please take care to avoid overcooking this one. Ideally, you want the fish to be dusky pink on the outside while retaining a glossy orange centre. Despite its robust colour this is a delicately flavoured fish which is complemented by light Asian flavours.

SERVES 6

1 ocean trout fillet, about 1 kg (2 lb 4 oz), skin on

1 tablespoon Chinese rice wine

1 pinch of ground white pepper, plus extra, to serve

3 tablespoons chicken stock

1 tablespoon light soy sauce

1 teaspoon caster (superfine) sugar

5 cm (2 inch) piece of ginger, shredded as finely as possible

6 spring onions (scallions), very thinly sliced

4 lime wedges, to serve

3 tablespoons vegetable oil

1 handful chopped coriander (cilantro), to serve

Put the fish on a baking tray. Rub the Chinese rice wine all over the fish and season with sea salt and the ground white pepper. Set aside for 30 minutes.

Tear off a large sheet of foil and lay on a work surface. Tear off a similar-sized sheet of baking paper and lay on top of the foil. Sit the fish in the centre.

Combine the stock, soy sauce and sugar in a small bowl to dissolve the sugar, then pour over the fish.

Scatter the ginger and half the spring onions over the fish. Loosely wrap the fish in the foil.

Your firepit is ready to cook on after about 2 hours of burning, when the timber is charcoal black, has transformed into red hot coals about the size of golf balls, and the smoke has all but subsided. To test for heat, you should not be able to hold the palm of your hand 5–10 cm (2–4 inches) above the grill for more than 2–3 seconds. Replace the grill over the firepit and give it around 10 minutes to heat up. (See page 9.)

Put the fish on the firepit grill and cook for 20 minutes. Leaving the fish wrapped, transfer to a serving platter.

Meanwhile, cook the lime, cut side down, on the firepit for 8–10 minutes until caramelised.

Put the oil in a small saucepan and sit the saucepan on the firepit. When the surface of the oil is shimmering and smoking hot, unwrap the fish and carefully pour the hot oil over the fish.

Scatter the remaining spring onion and the coriander on top and sprinkle with white pepper. Serve with lime wedges.

NEWSPAPER-WRAPPED SALMON WITH FRESH HERBS, LEMON AND CHILLI

Wetting the newspaper prevents it burning on the firepit (although it will scorch a little anyway, which is fine) and creates a steamy environment for the fish to cook in. This makes cooking for a crowd very easy. Only limited by the size of your firepit, you could easily cook six or eight of these and feed an army with little effort.

SERVES 4

2 salmon fillets, mid cut, about 400 g (14 oz) each

1 bunch spring onions (scallions)

1 large handful flat-leaf (Italian) parsley, roughly chopped

1 large handful coriander (cilantro) leaves, chopped

1 handful mint leaves, chopped

1 large red chilli, thinly sliced (seeded, if it's a hot one)

1 lemon, sliced

3 tablespoons olive oil

3 tablespoons lemon juice

1 teaspoon sea salt

Lay out 2 large sheets of newspaper on top of each other and liberally brush all over with water to dampen. Tear off 2 pieces of baking paper, slightly larger than each fish fillet and sit them in the middle of the newspaper.

Finely slice 3 spring onions and put in a bowl with the other herbs and the chilli. Cut the remaining spring onions in half, lengthways, and lay these on top of the baking paper. Now lay the lemon slices on the spring onions. Sit the fish on the lemons and season well with sea salt and freshly ground black pepper. Scatter the herb mix evenly over the fish.

Combine the olive oil and lemon juice and pour over the fish. Fold up the newspaper to form a parcel by bringing the long sides together and folding down. Tuck the two shorter ends in underneath. Set aside for 20 minutes.

Your firepit is ready to cook on after about 2 hours of burning, when the timber is charcoal black, has transformed into red hot coals about the size of golf balls, and the smoke has all but subsided. To test for heat, you should not be able to hold the palm of your hand 5–10 cm (2–4 inches) above the grill for more than 2–3 seconds. Replace the grill over the firepit and give it around 10 minutes to heat up. (See page 9.)

Put the fish parcel on the firepit grill. Cook for 15 minutes, until the fish is just cooked through. Cook for a further 5 minutes if you like salmon well done. Leave to rest for 5 minutes before carefully moving the fish to a plate. Drizzle with the cooking juices to serve.

TOFU AND SHIITAKE SKEWERS WITH GINGER DRESSING 146

LIME AND TURMERIC TOFU STEAKS WITH FRESH SAMBAL 149

ULTIMATE FIREPIT VEGIE SALAD 150

ZUCCHINI, EGGPLANT AND HALOUMI SKEWERS 153

MUSHROOMS WITH MARINATED FETA 154

SWEET POTATOES IN JACKETS WITH FETA CRÈME 157

FIREPIT BREAD AND TOMATO SALAD 158

LIME LEAF AND LEMONGRASS TOFU 161

PANEER SKEWERS WITH TOMATO RELISH 162

GRILLED COS WITH PARMESAN BUTTER 165

SPICY BARBECUED CORN 166

CHAKCHOUKA 169

FRAGRANT FIVE-SPICE VEGETABLE PARCELS 170

CHARRED TOMATO SALSA WITH CORN CHIPS 173

QUESADILLAS WITH PUMPKIN, PEPITAS AND MOZZARELLA 174

ISRAELI EGGPLANT SALAD 177

BAKED POTATOES WITH HERBED LABNEH 178

INDIAN SPICED EGGPLANT 181

GRILLED CORN WITH JALAPEÑO, LIME AND PARMESAN BUTTER 182

SWEET AND SOUR PUMPKIN 185

CHARGRILLED FENNEL WITH CHILLI AND HERBS 186

FIREPIT BARBIE GHANOUSH 189

VEGIES

TOFU AND SHIITAKE SKEWERS WITH GINGER DRESSING

The ginger and spring onion dressing can be made a day in advance. Store it in an airtight container in the fridge until needed, but allow it time to come back to room temperature before using.

SERVES 4

300 g (11 oz) firm tofu

24 truss cherry tomatoes

24 small shiitake mushrooms

1 tablespoon olive oil

2 teaspoons light soy sauce

1 handful coriander (cilantro) sprigs

GINGER AND SPRING ONION DRESSING

2 tablespoons julienned fresh young ginger

125 g (4½ oz) thinly sliced spring onions (scallions)

3 tablespoons vegetable oil

2 tablespoons light soy sauce

1 teaspoon sesame oil

To make the dressing, put the ginger and spring onions in a small bowl. Heat the oil in a small saucepan over high heat until smoking hot. Pour the hot oil over the ginger and spring onions so they sizzle and soften, then stir in the soy sauce and sesame oil. Set aside and prepare the skewers.

Use 8 metal or soaked bamboo skewers. Cut the tofu into pieces about the same size as the tomatoes. Thread tofu, 3 tomatoes and 3 mushrooms onto each skewer. Put the skewers in a flat dish. Combine the oil and soy sauce and brush over the skewers.

Your firepit is ready to cook on after about 2 hours of burning, when the timber is charcoal black, has transformed into red hot coals about the size of golf balls, and the smoke has all but subsided. To test for heat, you should not be able to hold the palm of your hand 5–10 cm (2–4 inches) above the grill for more than 2–3 seconds. Replace the grill over the firepit and give it around 10 minutes to heat up. (See page 9.)

Put a baking tray on the firepit grill and give it 10 minutes or so to heat up.

Put the skewers on the hot baking tray and cook for 12–15 minutes, turning every few minutes, until the tofu and vegetables are golden and tender. Transfer to a serving plate.

Spoon the dressing over the skewers. Serve scattered with coriander sprigs.

LIME AND TURMERIC TOFU STEAKS WITH FRESH SAMBAL

The real flavour in this recipe comes from the sambal, and as far as flavours go, you won't be left wanting. Sambal is a chilli-based condiment used throughout Southeast Asia. It is generally cooked, but this is a very raw, very fresh and very tasty version.

SERVES 4

600 g (1 lb 5 oz) firm tofu

3 tablespoons lime juice

3 tablespoons olive oil

¼ teaspoon ground turmeric

Lime wedges, to serve

FRESH SAMBAL

1 teaspoon vegetable stock (bouillon) powder

2 makrut lime leaves, thinly sliced

2 lemongrass stems, white part only, finely chopped

2 bird's eye chillies, finely chopped

3 tablespoons finely chopped red Asian shallots

2 garlic cloves, finely chopped

1 tablespoon vegetable oil

1 tablespoon lime juice

For the fresh sambal, combine the ingredients in a bowl and stir until the stock powder has dissolved. Cover and set aside for 30 minutes, or refrigerate overnight. Remove from the fridge 30 minutes before serving.

Cut the tofu into 4 equal portions. Place in a flat non-metallic dish in a single layer.

Combine the lime juice, oil and turmeric in a bowl and stir until the turmeric has dissolved and the oil is vibrantly coloured. Pour over the tofu and turn to coat all over. Set aside for 1 hour.

Your firepit is ready to cook on after about 2 hours of burning, when the timber is charcoal black, has transformed into red hot coals about the size of golf balls, and the smoke has all but subsided. To test for heat, you should not be able to hold the palm of your hand 5–10 cm (2–4 inches) above the grill for more than 2–3 seconds. Replace the grill over the firepit and give it around 10 minutes to heat up. (See page 9.)

Cook the tofu on the firepit grill for 4–5 minutes on each side, until golden. Serve with the lime wedges on the side and the sambal in a bowl to spoon over the tofu.

ULTIMATE FIREPIT VEGIE SALAD

This is a very simple, very tasty recipe to have in your repertoire. Start with a few basics: chopped garlic, chilli, parsley, some sort of oil and something with a tang factor (like vinegar or lemon juice). Then simply add whatever barbecued vegies you like. In summer I am partial to vine vegies — eggplant, tomatoes and beans. Get them all charred-up and tasty.

SERVES 4

8 small roma (plum) tomatoes, halved lengthways

3 tablespoons olive oil

1 large eggplant (aubergine), cut into large chunks

500 g (1 lb 2 oz) green beans

1 red onion, finely sliced

1 handful dill, chopped

1 handful basil leaves, chopped

1 handful flat-leaf (Italian) parsley, chopped

DRESSING

4 garlic cloves, finely chopped

2 large red chillies, finely chopped

1 small handful chopped flat-leaf (Italian) parsley

½ cup (125 ml) olive oil

3 tablespoons sherry vinegar

1 teaspoon sea salt

Combine the dressing ingredients in a bowl and leave to infuse.

Your firepit is ready to cook on after about 2 hours of burning, when the timber is charcoal black, has transformed into red hot coals about the size of golf balls, and the smoke has all but subsided. To test for heat, you should not be able to hold the palm of your hand 5–10 cm (2–4 inches) above the grill for more than 2–3 seconds. Replace the grill over the firepit and give it around 10 minutes to heat up. (See page 9.)

Cook the vegies one variety at a time.

Put the tomatoes in a large bowl. Add about one-third of the olive oil, season well with salt and pepper and toss the tomatoes in the oil. Put the tomatoes, cut side down, on the firepit grill for a few minutes — just long enough for them to form grill marks. Don't overcook them. Turn them and cook for 2–3 more minutes. Remove to a large bowl.

Put the eggplant in the same bowl you tossed the tomatoes in. Add another third of the olive oil and season well with salt and pepper. Toss the eggplant to coat in oil. Put the eggplant on the firepit grill and cook for 10 minutes, turning often, until golden and tender. Put in the bowl with the tomatoes.

Finally, put the beans into the bowl, add the remaining olive oil and season well with salt and pepper. Toss the beans well and lay them carefully on the grill (don't let them fall through the cracks). Cook for 8–10 minutes, turning often, until nicely charred. Add to the bowl of eggplant and tomatoes.

Spoon some of the dressing over the warm vegies. Give a quick toss and season to taste. Stir in the red onion, dill, basil and parsley. Add the remaining dressing and serve warm or at room temperature.

ZUCCHINI, EGGPLANT AND HALOUMI SKEWERS

Haloumi is one of those ingredients that seemed to appear from out of nowhere to become one of our favourite things to cook. Here, it is cubed and skewered with eggplant and zucchini.

SERVES 4

500 g (1 lb 2 oz) haloumi cheese

2 Japanese eggplants (aubergines)

2 zucchini (courgettes)

2 tablespoons olive oil, plus extra, for brushing

2 tablespoons apple cider vinegar

2 teaspoons cumin seeds

1 teaspoon dried chilli flakes

Soak 8 bamboo skewers in cold water for an hour.

Cut the haloumi, eggplant and zucchini into 2 cm (¾ inch) chunks. Thread alternately onto the skewers. Lay the skewers in a flat non-metallic dish.

Mix together the olive oil, vinegar, cumin and chilli and pour over the skewers. Cover and leave at room temperature for a couple of hours to allow the flavours to infuse.

Your firepit is ready to cook on after about 2 hours of burning, when the timber is charcoal black, has transformed into red hot coals about the size of golf balls, and the smoke has all but subsided. To test for heat, you should not be able to hold the palm of your hand 5–10 cm (2–4 inches) above the grill for more than 2–3 seconds. Replace the grill over the firepit and give it around 10 minutes to heat up. (See page 9.)

Put the skewers on the firepit grill (keep the marinade) and cook for 2–3 minutes until the haloumi is golden. Turn over and cook for another 2 minutes.

Drizzle with the remaining marinade to serve.

MUSHROOMS WITH MARINATED FETA

Mushrooms, and most specifically big ones, are ideal for the firepit. They lend themselves to all sorts of cooking techniques and pair well with many different flavours. The marinated feta can be made a few days in advance. Just spoon the ready-marinated cheese into the mushroom caps and you're ready to cook. Easy.

SERVES 4

200 g (7 oz) semi-soft goat's feta cheese

2 thyme sprigs

2 garlic cloves, sliced

2 spring onions (scallions), finely sliced

½ cup (125 ml) light olive oil

½ teaspoon sea salt

2 tablespoons sherry vinegar

8 large field mushrooms, or pine mushrooms, if available

1 teaspoon sumac

Cut the feta into small bite-sized cubes and put in a bowl.

Put the thyme, garlic and spring onions in a heatproof bowl. Heat the olive oil in a small frying pan over medium heat. When the oil is smoking hot, pour it over the spring onions — they should sizzle in the oil and release their flavours. Stir in the salt, vinegar and ground black pepper to taste. Spoon over the feta. Cover and leave in the fridge for up to 3 days.

Your firepit is ready to cook on after about 2 hours of burning, when the timber is charcoal black, has transformed into red hot coals about the size of golf balls, and the smoke has all but subsided. To test for heat, you should not be able to hold the palm of your hand 5–10 cm (2–4 inches) above the grill for more than 2–3 seconds. Replace the grill over the firepit and give it around 10 minutes to heat up. (See page 9.)

Remove the stems from the mushrooms and spoon some feta and marinade into the caps. Sit the mushrooms on the firepit grill. Cook for 10–15 minutes, or until tender. If the mushrooms start to burn, move to the edge of the firepit where the heat is less intense.

Serve the mushrooms warm, sprinkled with the sumac.

SWEET POTATOES IN JACKETS WITH FETA CRÈME

Sweet potatoes, popular because they are low on the GI index and also taste so good, are the ideal vegie to cook on the firepit. They require little preparation and don't even need to be peeled. Their sweetness pairs well with tangy feta, herbs and chilli. Another advantage of these beauties is that you can cook enough to feed an army.

SERVES 4

4 sweet potatoes, about 300 g (11 oz) each

1 tablespoon olive oil

1 teaspoon sea salt

1 large red chilli, finely chopped,

4 dill sprigs

FETA CRÈME

300 g (11 oz) feta, coarsely grated or crumbled

1 garlic clove, crushed

1 tablespoon finely chopped dill

3 tablespoons olive oil

2 tablespoons milk

To make the feta crème, put the feta, garlic and dill in a food processor. Mix for about 10 seconds, until well combined. With the motor running, add the oil, then the milk, to make a smooth and creamy sauce. Transfer to a bowl and refrigerate until ready to use. This can be made a day or two in advance and kept in the fridge, where it will thicken.

Sit each of the sweet potatoes in the centre of a sheet of foil. Rub with oil and sprinkle with sea salt. Wrap in the foil to firmly enclose.

Your firepit is ready to cook on after about 2 hours of burning, when the timber is charcoal black, has transformed into red hot coals about the size of golf balls, and the smoke has all but subsided. To test for heat, you should not be able to hold the palm of your hand 5–10 cm (2–4 inches) above the grill for more than 2–3 seconds. Replace the grill over the firepit and give it around 10 minutes to heat up. (See page 9.)

Sit the sweet potatoes on the firepit grill and cook for 45–60 minutes, until they can easily be pierced with a skewer. Avoid unwrapping the foil before they are cooked or the heat will escape.

To serve, unwrap the sweet potatoes and make a deep cut down the centre of each. Spoon the feta crème into the potatoes and top with chopped chilli, a sprig of dill and some ground black pepper.

FIREPIT BREAD AND TOMATO SALAD

This is my firepit take on panzanella — that classic Tuscan summer vegetable and bread salad — but it can be made year round. Be sure to leave your tomatoes at room temperature for several days, or even a week, before using, to improve their flavour.

SERVES 4

4 thick slices ciabatta or sourdough bread

6 ripe tomatoes, chopped

2 red onions, chopped

½ cup (15 g) roughly chopped flat-leaf (Italian) parsley

DRESSING

3 tablespoons extra virgin olive oil

3 tablespoons apple cider vinegar

1 teaspoon sea salt

1 teaspoon dried oregano

1 garlic clove, crushed

To make the dressing, combine all the ingredients in a bowl.

Your firepit is ready to cook on after about 2 hours of burning, when the timber is charcoal black, has transformed into red hot coals about the size of golf balls, and the smoke has all but subsided. To test for heat, you should not be able to hold the palm of your hand 5–10 cm (2–4 inches) above the grill for more than 2–3 seconds. Replace the grill over the firepit and give it around 10 minutes to heat up. (See page 9.)

Lay the bread on the firepit grill and cook until toasted and charred on both sides, turning once. Remove to a bowl. Allow to cool a little.

When the bread is cool enough to handle, tear into chunks in the bowl. Add the tomatoes, onion and parsley. Pour in the dressing and toss before serving.

LIME LEAF AND LEMONGRASS TOFU

I can totally understand if you think you don't particularly like tofu — it is often cooked really badly. I mean, if you cooked a fillet steak for 20 minutes on each side, I probably wouldn't like that either! Tofu is a chameleon of sorts that takes on the flavours it is cooked with. So, when cooked well (and by this, I generally mean simply and quickly) and used with other flavours, you will understand why tofu is no longer only enjoyed by vegetarians. If you can't get your hands on kecap manis, soy sauce with a little brown sugar will do the job nicely.

SERVES 4

2 lemongrass stalks, white part only, chopped

2 garlic cloves, chopped

2 makrut lime leaves, thinly sliced

1 tablespoon finely grated ginger

2 tablespoons fish sauce

2 tablespoons vegetable oil

1 teaspoon caster (superfine) sugar

300 g (11 oz) block of firm tofu

Kecap manis, to serve

Coriander (cilantro) sprigs, to serve

Put the lemongrass, garlic, lime leaves, ginger, fish sauce, vegetable oil and sugar in a food processor and blend to make a chunky sauce. Transfer to a bowl and add the tofu. Gently turn the tofu to evenly cover. Set aside at room temperature for a couple of hours.

Your firepit is ready to cook on after about 2 hours of burning, when the timber is charcoal black, has transformed into red hot coals about the size of golf balls, and the smoke has all but subsided. To test for heat, you should not be able to hold the palm of your hand 5–10 cm (2–4 inches) above the grill for more than 2–3 seconds. Replace the grill over the firepit and give it around 10 minutes to heat up. (See page 9.)

Put the block of tofu on the firepit grill and cook for 5 minutes. Turn the tofu over (the lemongrass mixture will have cooked golden and charred in some places). Cook for another 5 minutes.

Cut into large cubes, drizzle with kecap manis and scatter with coriander to serve.

PANEER SKEWERS WITH TOMATO RELISH

Paneer is an Indian 'cheese', though not what Westerners would call cheese. It is a fresh cheese and does not use a setting agent. Have you ever left fresh ricotta in the fridge for several days? It becomes very firm, just like paneer — which, by the way, is so good in curries too.

SERVES 4

400 g (14 oz) block of paneer (Indian cottage cheese)

Lemon wedges, to serve

SPICE SEASONING

3 tablespoons rice bran oil

2 teaspoons dried thyme

2 teaspoons dried oregano

2 teaspoons smoked paprika

1 teaspoon cayenne pepper

1 teaspoon sea salt

TOMATO RELISH

2 roma (plum) tomatoes, finely diced

1 small red onion, finely diced

2 teaspoons soft brown sugar

2 tablespoons lime juice

½ teaspoon celery seeds

¼ teaspoon nigella seeds

Combine the spice seasoning ingredients in a flat dish.

Cut the paneer into 8 rectangles, about the size of fat chips. Roll each chip in the seasoning to coat all over. Cover and leave in the fridge for several hours.

Soak 8 bamboo skewers in cold water for an hour.

Combine all the tomato relish ingredients in a bowl and leave for the flavours to develop.

Your firepit is ready to cook on after about 2 hours of burning, when the timber is charcoal black, has transformed into red hot coals about the size of golf balls, and the smoke has all but subsided. To test for heat, you should not be able to hold the palm of your hand 5–10 cm (2–4 inches) above the grill for more than 2–3 seconds. Replace the grill over the firepit and give it around 10 minutes to heat up. (See page 9.)

Thread a bamboo skewer through each piece of paneer. Cook the skewers on the firepit grill for 8–10 minutes, turning every couple of minutes, until dark coloured and aromatic. Serve immediately, with the tomato relish and lemon wedges.

GRILLED COS WITH PARMESAN BUTTER

It might seem odd to grill a lettuce. But little cos have more robust leaves than other lettuce varieties and can stand up to a good chargrilling. Make the butter in advance and this one is so easy to throw together and serve with some fish or chicken cooked on the firepit.

SERVES 4

4 baby cos lettuce

1 tablespoon olive oil

55 g (2 oz) finely grated parmesan cheese, to serve

PARMESAN BUTTER

85 g (3 oz) unsalted butter, softened

55 g (2 oz) finely grated parmesan cheese

1 garlic clove, crushed

1 tablespoon finely chopped flat-leaf (Italian) parsley

1 tablespoon finely chopped tarragon

To make the parmesan butter, mix together the butter, parmesan, garlic, parsley and tarragon in a bowl. Season with salt and freshly ground black pepper. This can be made a day or two in advance and kept in the fridge — bring it to room temperature before you start to cook.

Cut each cos lengthways through the middle. Rub or brush olive oil over the cut side of the cos.

Your firepit is ready to cook on after about 2 hours of burning, when the timber is charcoal black, has transformed into red hot coals about the size of golf balls, and the smoke has all but subsided. To test for heat, you should not be able to hold the palm of your hand 5–10 cm (2–4 inches) above the grill for more than 2–3 seconds. Replace the grill over the firepit and give it around 10 minutes to heat up. (See page 9.)

Cook the cos, cut side down, on the firepit grill for 3–4 minutes, until charred. Remove from the grill.

Spread the butter over the grilled side of the cos and return to the grill, cut side up. Cook for 2–3 minutes, until the butter softens and melts into the lettuce.

Scatter with parmesan to serve.

SPICY BARBECUED CORN

Mother Nature created corn for the firepit. Well, that's how it feels. Sweet corn only gets sweeter when it is grilled and the sugars caramelise. To offset and complement the sweetness, the grilled corn is finished off with the umami flavours of manchego, feta and fragrant smoked paprika.

SERVES 4

3 tablespoons mayonnaise

1 teaspoon smoked paprika

½ teaspoon dried chilli flakes

4 fresh corn cobs

2 tablespoons softened butter

55 g (2 oz) manchego cheese, finely grated

55 g (2 oz) firm feta, coarsely grated

1 tablespoon finely chopped coriander (cilantro)

Lime wedges, to serve

Mix together the mayonnaise, paprika and chilli flakes.

Your firepit is ready to cook on after about 2 hours of burning, when the timber is charcoal black, has transformed into red hot coals about the size of golf balls, and the smoke has all but subsided. To test for heat, you should not be able to hold the palm of your hand 5–10 cm (2–4 inches) above the grill for more than 2–3 seconds. Replace the grill over the firepit and give it around 10 minutes to heat up. (See page 9.)

Put the corn on the firepit grill and cook for 12–15 minutes, turning often and brushing with the softened butter until the kernels start to char.

Transfer to a serving plate. Spoon the mayonnaise over each cob, then sprinkle with the cheeses and coriander. Serve with lime wedges on the side.

CHAKCHOUKA

Translating Arabic to English can be tricky, which is why, in the world of food, you often see the names of Middle Eastern dishes spelt in different ways. That's how it is with this fabulously flavoursome dish from North Africa, also called shakshouka. I consider this the vegetarian equivalent to bacon and eggs as hangover food. The name alone makes you want to sit up and take notice.

SERVES 4

3 tablespoons vegetable oil

6 ripe tomatoes, cut in half

1 small yellow capsicum (pepper), cut into strips

1 small green capsicum (pepper), cut into strips

1 small red capsicum (pepper), cut into strips

1 red onion, cut into rings

1 large red chilli, finely chopped

1 teaspoon ground cumin

1 teaspoon sweet paprika

1 teaspoon sea salt

4 eggs

3 tablespoons finely chopped flat-leaf (Italian) parsley

Chargrilled bread, to serve

Your firepit is ready to cook on after about 2 hours of burning, when the timber is charcoal black, has transformed into red hot coals about the size of golf balls, and the smoke has all but subsided. To test for heat, you should not be able to hold the palm of your hand 5–10 cm (2–4 inches) above the grill for more than 2–3 seconds. Replace the grill over the firepit and give it around 10 minutes to heat up. (See page 9.)

Put the oil in a large bowl. Add the tomatoes, capsicums and onion and toss the vegies around to coat in the oil.

Working in batches, tumble some of the vegies over the firepit grill and spread them around so they don't overlap. Cook for 8–10 minutes, turning often with metal tongs until they are tender and scored with grill marks. Transfer to a bowl and cook the remaining vegetables.

Sprinkle the cooked vegetables with chilli, cumin, paprika and salt and toss together. Lightly mash with a potato masher, so the tomatoes especially are well crushed. Spoon onto a heavy-based baking tray.

Put the tray on the firepit grill and allow to heat up for 10 minutes. Form 4 evenly spaced little wells in the tomato mixture, then crack an egg into each one.

Cook for 8–10 minutes, just until the egg whites are firm. Sprinkle with parsley and serve hot with chargrilled bread.

FRAGRANT FIVE-SPICE VEGETABLE PARCELS

Fresh shiitake mushrooms have such a wonderful savoury aroma. Dried shiitakes are even more intense and also work well for this recipe: they store well, are inexpensive and easy to use. Just put them in a bowl, pour in enough boiling water to cover them and leave to soften for about 30 minutes. Then discard the stems and either use the caps whole or chop them up. This dish is great served with steamed brown rice.

SERVES 4

12 shiitake mushrooms, stems removed

1 small sweet potato, cut into rounds 1 cm (½ inch) thick

200 g (7 oz) peeled daikon, cut into 2.5 cm (1 inch) cubes

200 g (7 oz) firm tofu, cut into 2.5 cm (1 inch) pieces

2 tablespoons thinly sliced shiso leaves

3 tablespoons soy sauce

1 tablespoon mirin

½ teaspoon sugar

½ teaspoon Chinese five-spice

1 teaspoon sesame oil

Combine all the ingredients in a large bowl. Tear off a sheet of foil about 30 cm (12 inches) square and place a similar-sized piece of baking paper over the foil.

Spoon a quarter of the vegie mixture in the middle of the baking paper. Bring the sides of the foil up to enclose the vegetables, and then seal the edges together. Repeat to make 4 parcels.

Your firepit is ready to cook on after about 2 hours of burning, when the timber is charcoal black, has transformed into red hot coals about the size of golf balls, and the smoke has all but subsided. To test for heat, you should not be able to hold the palm of your hand 5–10 cm (2–4 inches) above the grill for more than 2–3 seconds. Replace the grill over the firepit and give it around 10 minutes to heat up. (See page 9.)

Sit the parcels on the firepit grill and cook for 12–15 minutes, until the vegetables are tender and aromatic. Serve hot.

CHARRED TOMATO SALSA WITH CORN CHIPS

The idea for this came from making something very similar as a sauce to spoon over grilled fish and chicken. Feel free to try this. It tastes so good and can be eaten by the spoonful. So much so that I found myself dipping in corn chips to scoop up like a dip. Which is what it has become. It does require you running inside to use a food processor but this really only takes a couple of minutes and is well worth the small effort.

SERVES 4

4 large ripe tomatoes

2 large green chillies

4 garlic cloves, peeled

4 French shallots

2 tablespoons rice vinegar

1 teaspoon caster (superfine) sugar

½ teaspoon sea salt

1 small handful coriander (cilantro) leaves and stems, roughly chopped

Corn chips, to serve

Your firepit is ready to cook on after about 2 hours of burning, when the timber is charcoal black, has transformed into red hot coals about the size of golf balls, and the smoke has all but subsided. To test for heat, you should not be able to hold the palm of your hand 5–10 cm (2–4 inches) above the grill for more than 2–3 seconds. Replace the grill over the firepit and give it around 10 minutes to heat up. (See page 9.)

Put a large baking tray on the firepit grill and give it about 10 minutes to heat up. The idea here is to cook each of the vegetables until the skins are nicely charred, adding flavour to the salsa.

Put the tomatoes, chillies, garlic and shallots on the hot baking tray. Some of the vegies will cook quicker than others. Simply keep turning them every few minutes. When the skin is charred all over, remove to a chopping board. Roughly pick off and discard the burnt bits, but don't be too fussy here as you want some of these well-cooked bits of skin in the salsa.

Cut the tomatoes in half and squeeze out the juice. Put the tomatoes in a food processor. Roughly chop the chillies, garlic and shallots and add to the food processor. Process to a chunky paste. Pour into a bowl and add the rice vinegar, sugar, salt and coriander. Taste and add more salt if needed.

Serve with corn chips.

QUESADILLAS WITH PUMPKIN, PEPITAS AND MOZZARELLA

These are ideal to kickstart a firepit fiesta, possibly with a crisp Mexican beer or classic lime-spiked margarita. Quesadillas are great for feeding a crowd: you could literally make a stack of these. They keep really well in the fridge and the options for fillings are almost limitless. This version is but a mere tasty suggestion.

SERVES 4—8

800 g (1 lb 12 oz) pumpkin, peeled, chopped into 2.5 cm (1 inch) pieces

3 tablespoons olive oil

2 teaspoons ground cumin

2 teaspoons smoked paprika

1 teaspoon garlic powder

1 teaspoon sea salt

1 tablespoon sliced jalapeños in brine, drained and chopped

8 burritos

100 g (3½ oz) coarsely grated mozzarella cheese

55 g (2 oz) coarsely grated feta cheese

55 g (2 oz) pepitas (pumpkin seeds), lightly toasted

To make the filling, preheat the oven to 180°C (350°F) and line a tray with baking paper.

Put the pumpkin, oil, cumin, paprika, garlic powder and salt in a bowl and toss well. Tumble the pumpkin onto the tray and bake for 30—35 minutes, until very soft. Put the pumpkin and cooking juices into a bowl and mash to a chunky paste. Stir in the jalapeno.

Lay 4 burritos on a work surface. Spread with the pumpkin filling. Scatter mozzarella, feta and then the pepitas over each burrito. Put the other 4 burritos on top. (These can be wrapped in plastic and kept in the fridge for 1 day now.)

Your firepit is ready to cook on after about 2 hours of burning, when the timber is charcoal black, has transformed into red hot coals about the size of golf balls, and the smoke has all but subsided. To test for heat, you should not be able to hold the palm of your hand 5—10 cm (2—4 inches) above the grill for more than 2—3 seconds. Replace the grill over the firepit and give it around 10 minutes to heat up. (See page 9.)

Lay the quesadillas on the firepit grill and cook for 3—4 minutes on each side, until golden and toasted.

Transfer to a chopping board and cut into wedges to serve.

ISRAELI EGGPLANT SALAD

If you're ever looking for a decent reference book on cooking vegies, try to get your hands on a copy of Mollie Katzen's *The Enchanted Broccoli Forest*. In the 1980s it was in the kitchen of just about every student. It is a well-worn and much-loved book on my shelf and was the inspiration for this delicious recipe.

SERVES 4

2 eggplants (aubergines)

4 truss tomatoes

1 handful coriander (cilantro)

1 handful chopped flat-leaf (Italian) parsley

SPICY LEMON DRESSING

3 tablespoons olive oil

3 tablespoons lemon juice

2 teaspoons ground cumin

2 teaspoons hot paprika

½ teaspoon cayenne pepper

Your firepit is ready to cook on after about 2 hours of burning, when the timber is charcoal black, has transformed into red hot coals about the size of golf balls, and the smoke has all but subsided. To test for heat, you should not be able to hold the palm of your hand 5–10 cm (2–4 inches) above the grill for more than 2–3 seconds. Replace the grill over the firepit and give it around 10 minutes to heat up. (See page 9.)

Sit the eggplant and tomatoes on the firepit grill. When they start to smoke, give them a turn. Continue until the vegies look charred all over, then remove from the grill.

When cool enough to handle, peel off the eggplant skins and discard — there's no need to be too fussy about removing all the burnt bits, as these add flavour. Tear the flesh of the eggplant into long lengths and place in a bowl.

Peel and discard the tomato skins. Chop the flesh and add to the eggplant, along with any seeds and juice. Don't mix them together at this stage.

Put the dressing ingredients in a bowl and stir to combine. Pour the dressing over the vegetables and use a large spoon to gently coat all the vegies — you don't want to break them up too much.

Stir in the herbs and season well with sea salt and ground black pepper. Serve warm, or at room temperature.

BAKED POTATOES WITH HERBED LABNEH

Go and get some labneh and try it, please. And then use it in all kinds of dishes, as a substitute for all sorts of other things. Try it in dips instead of sour cream. Use it as you would hummus — or yoghurt, which is what it is anyway. You can even use labneh to replace ricotta or cream cheese in sweets such as cheesecake.

SERVES 4

4 large potatoes, unpeeled but washed

HERBED LABNEH

½ cup (125 g) labneh (strained yoghurt cheese)

1 tablespoon snipped chives

1 tablespoon finely chopped flat-leaf (Italian) parsley

1 tablespoon finely chopped mint

For the herbed labneh, mix together all the ingredients. Cover and leave at room temperature.

Your firepit is ready to cook on after about 2 hours of burning, when the timber is charcoal black, has transformed into red hot coals about the size of golf balls, and the smoke has all but subsided. To test for heat, you should not be able to hold the palm of your hand 5–10 cm (2–4 inches) above the grill for more than 2–3 seconds. Replace the grill over the firepit and give it around 10 minutes to heat up. (See page 9.)

Wrap each potato in foil. Sit them on the firepit grill and cook for 1 hour. The potatoes are cooked through when you can easily pierce them with a skewer.

Remove the potatoes from the grill and leave them in their foil for 10–15 minutes. (You can leave them on the edge of the firepit to keep warm.)

Unwrap the potatoes, then press down on them gently with a potato masher or spatula to flatten and split the skin.

Spoon the herbed labneh into the hot potatoes and serve.

INDIAN SPICED EGGPLANT

Take note of this method of adding seasoning and flavour to just-cooked eggplant. The heat of the eggplant releases the fragrant oil in the spices. Eggplant is a highly absorbent vegie — you'll notice how much oil it sucks up when being fried.

SERVES 4–6

2 eggplants (aubergines)

3 teaspoons sea salt

3 tablespoons olive oil

1 garlic clove, crushed

1 teaspoon ground cumin

½ teaspoon chilli powder

1 handful mint leaves, torn

½ cup (125 g) labneh (strained yoghurt cheese)

Your firepit is ready to cook on after about 2 hours of burning, when the timber is charcoal black, has transformed into red hot coals about the size of golf balls, and the smoke has all but subsided. To test for heat, you should not be able to hold the palm of your hand 5–10 cm (2–4 inches) above the grill for more than 2–3 seconds. Replace the grill over the firepit and give it around 10 minutes to heat up. (See page 9.)

Cut the eggplant lengthways into large wedges. Place in a bowl with the salt and about half the oil and toss to coat. Tumble the eggplant onto the firepit grill and then cook for 12–15 minutes, using tongs to spread the wedges out and turn often until golden and just tender. Transfer to a bowl.

Combine the remaining oil, garlic, cumin and chilli powder in a small bowl. Pour over the eggplant while it is still hot, then gently toss to coat. Serve warm, scattered with mint, with the labneh on the side.

GRILLED CORN WITH JALAPEÑO, LIME AND PARMESAN BUTTER

It might sound odd, but the parmesan really does work a treat with the bite and tang of the other ingredients. It actually complements them. Because there are so few ingredients here, quality is the key: good butter, and good cheese.

SERVES 4

4 corn cobs, each cut into 3 smaller rounds

Lime wedges, to serve

JALAPEÑO, LIME AND PARMESAN BUTTER

125 g (4½ oz) unsalted butter, softened to room temperature

2 tablespoons sliced jalapeños in brine, drained

1 tablespoon lime juice

¼ cup (25 g) finely grated parmesan cheese

For the jalapeño, lime and parmesan butter, put all the ingredients in a food processor and whiz until smooth. Scrape into a bowl, then cover and refrigerate until needed. This can be kept in the fridge for 2–3 weeks.

Your firepit is ready to cook on after about 2 hours of burning, when the timber is charcoal black, has transformed into red hot coals about the size of golf balls, and the smoke has all but subsided. To test for heat, you should not be able to hold the palm of your hand 5–10 cm (2–4 inches) above the grill for more than 2–3 seconds. Replace the grill over the firepit and give it around 10 minutes to heat up. (See page 9.)

Cook the corn on the firepit grill for about 15 minutes, turning often, until the kernels are dark and caramelised.

Remove the hot corn cobs to a bowl, add the jalapeño butter and toss together well. Serve with lime wedges.

SWEET AND SOUR PUMPKIN

Sweet and sour is not a flavour combination unique to Chinese cooking. The Sicilians are masters of it too, albeit in a much more subtle way. This combination of sugar and vinegar is common in Southern Italian cooking.

SERVES 4

1 small jap or kent pumpkin (winter squash)

2 tablespoons olive oil

DRESSING

4 tablespoons red wine vinegar

3 tablespoons olive oil

2 garlic cloves, finely chopped

¼ teaspoon dried chilli flakes

2 teaspoons soft brown sugar

1 large handful mint leaves, roughly chopped

3 tablespoons currants

Cut the pumpkin in half with a large knife. Scoop out and discard the seeds with a large metal spoon. Lay the cut side of the pumpkin flat on a chopping board. Cut the pumpkin into thick wedges, following the natural indentations.

Place the pumpkin in a bowl with the oil, and season well with sea salt and freshly ground black pepper.

Combine the dressing ingredients in a bowl, mixing to dissolve the sugar.

Your firepit is ready to cook on after about 2 hours of burning, when the timber is charcoal black, has transformed into red hot coals about the size of golf balls, and the smoke has all but subsided. To test for heat, you should not be able to hold the palm of your hand 5–10 cm (2–4 inches) above the grill for more than 2–3 seconds. Replace the grill over the firepit and give it around 10 minutes to heat up. (See page 9.)

Lay the pumpkin wedges on the firepit grill, cut side down, and cook for 10 minutes. Turn the pumpkin over and cook for another 5–10 minutes. Now move the pumpkin to the edge of the firepit where the heat is less intense and cook for a further 20 minutes, turning often until just cooked through and tender, but retaining some firmness.

Place the hot pumpkin in a large bowl. Pour the dressing over the top, toss to combine, and season to taste. Serve warm, or at room temperature.

CHARGRILLED FENNEL WITH CHILLI AND HERBS

Fennel in all its forms is delicious. The feathery tops add flavour to dressings and mayonnaise. The beefy bulbs can be cooked in all sorts of ways — in pasta sauces, risotto, minestrone, and roasted with pork or chicken. Fennel seeds are a staple in my cupboard, ready to be used in both Indian- and Italian-inspired recipes.

SERVES 4

4 fennel bulbs, preferably with fronds

2 garlic cloves, chopped

3 tablespoons olive oil

2 tablespoons red wine vinegar

2 teaspoons dijon mustard

½ teaspoon sea salt

Dried chilli flakes, to taste

1 handful flat-leaf (Italian) parsley leaves, finely chopped

1 handful mint leaves, finely chopped

If the fennel has feathery fronds, cut these off and roughly chop up enough to give a small handful.

Cut the fennel lengthways into slices 5 mm (¼ inch) thick. Place in a bowl with the garlic and 1 tablespoon olive oil. Set aside at room temperature for 30 minutes to infuse.

In a large bowl, combine the remaining olive oil with the remaining ingredients to make a herb dressing.

Your firepit is ready to cook on after about 2 hours of burning, when the timber is charcoal black, has transformed into red hot coals about the size of golf balls, and the smoke has all but subsided. To test for heat, you should not be able to hold the palm of your hand 5–10 cm (2–4 inches) above the grill for more than 2–3 seconds. Replace the grill over the firepit and give it around 10 minutes to heat up. (See page 9.)

Tumble half the fennel over the firepit grill and spread the slices out so they don't overlap. Cook for 4–5 minutes on each side, until the fennel is golden and charred and the garlic is golden and aromatic. Add the hot fennel to the bowl of herb dressing and toss to coat. Cook the remaining fennel in the same way and add to the dressing.

Serve warm or at room temperature, sprinkled with any reserved fennel fronds.

FIREPIT BARBIE GHANOUSH

This one is made for the firepit. Actually, I don't believe you can achieve the same flavour without cooking the eggplant over a naked flame. The smokiness of the charred skin somehow gets into the flesh of the eggplant with really very little cooking time.

SERVES 6–8

2 large eggplants (aubergines)

2 teaspoons sea salt

3 tablespoons lemon juice

3 garlic cloves, crushed

2 tablespoons extra virgin olive oil, plus extra, for drizzling

Chargrilled Middle Eastern flatbread, to serve

Your firepit is ready to cook on after about 2 hours of burning, when the timber is charcoal black, has transformed into red hot coals about the size of golf balls, and the smoke has all but subsided. To test for heat, you should not be able to hold the palm of your hand 5–10 cm (2–4 inches) above the grill for more than 2–3 seconds. Replace the grill over the firepit and give it around 10 minutes to heat up. (See page 9.)

Prick each eggplant several times with a fork. Cook them on the firepit grill for 10–15 minutes, turning often, until collapsed and tender. Remove and leave to cool on a tray.

When cool enough to handle, peel off and discard the skin of each eggplant. Place the flesh in a sieve over a bowl and set aside for 15 minutes to drain.

Put the eggplant flesh in a food processor with the salt, lemon juice, garlic and olive oil. Whiz to a purée, then pour the mixture into a bowl and drizzle with a little more olive oil.

Serve at room temperature, with chargrilled flatbread. This will keep in the fridge for 2–3 days.

NAM JIM (SWEET CHILLI SAUCE)...........192

FIREPIT WEDGES...........................193

ARABIAN SPICE MIX.................................194

EASY BEARNAISE SAUCE.........................195

MUHUMARRA..................................196

REAL GARLIC BREAD...............................197

FIREPIT DAMPER..198

TZATZIKI...199

BITS AND BOBS

NAM JIM (SWEET CHILLI SAUCE)

This is the sweet chilli sauce that's described as nam jim on a Thai menu. The ingredients are all very easy to track down and the end result really is a very authentic-tasting sweet chilli sauce that can sit on the table in a bowl and be enjoyed by the spoonful.

SERVES 4

6 coriander (cilantro) roots and stems, finely chopped
4 garlic cloves, chopped
2 large red chillies, chopped
1½ cups (375 ml) white vinegar
2 cups (440 g) sugar

Pound the coriander roots, garlic, chilli and a generous pinch of salt with a mortar and pestle into a murky-looking paste.

Put the vinegar and sugar in a pan with 375 ml (13 fl oz) water and bring to the boil, stirring to dissolve the sugar.

Add the paste and reduce the heat to a steady but rapid simmer for 10–15 minutes until syrupy. Pour into sterilised jars and leave to cool before sealing. Keep refrigerated.

FIREPIT WEDGES

Don't we all love potato chips? Especially when we're sitting around the firepit. Don't be tempted to constantly turn these on the hotplate, however much you're being badgered by your hungry mates.

SERVES 4

6 potatoes such as desiree, peeled and cut into 6–8 wedges each

2 tablespoons light olive oil

1 tablespoon celery salt, plus extra, to serve

Put the potato into a pan of boiling water, cover with a lid and turn off the heat. Leave to sit for 10 minutes. Drain well, then leave the potato on a clean tea towel to dry and cool.

Put the potato in a bowl with half the oil and the celery salt and toss well to coat.

Your firepit is ready to cook on after about 2 hours of burning, when the timber is charcoal black, has transformed into red hot coals about the size of golf balls, and the smoke has all but subsided. To test for heat, you should not be able to hold the palm of your hand 5–10 cm (2–4 inches) above the grill for more than 2–3 seconds. Replace the grill over the firepit and give it around 10 minutes to heat up. (See page 9.)

Put a baking tray on the firepit grill. Leave for 10 minutes or so to heat up. Drizzle the remaining oil over the baking tray.

Tumble the potato wedges onto the tray, spreading them around so they don't overlap. You want the potatoes to sizzle. If they look like they are cooking too quickly, simply move the tray closer to the edge of the firepit where the heat is less intense.

Cook for about 5 minutes each side until they start to turn golden. Sprinkle with extra celery salt and sea salt to taste. Serve hot.

ARABIAN SPICE MIX

This is my simplified version of za'atar, a Middle Eastern spice blend. Okay, so this spice mix isn't actually cooked on the firepit, but it's such a great accompaniment to grilled meats and poultry and vegies that I just had to include it. It's also very delicious sprinkled over chargrilled flatbreads dipped in olive oil.

SERVES 4

2 tablespoons sesame seeds

2 tablespoons dried thyme

2 tablespoons sumac

1 teaspoon sea salt

Put the sesame seeds in a small dry frying pan over medium heat. Cook, shaking the pan regularly, until evenly golden. Tip into a bowl and leave to cool.

Put the sesame seeds, thyme, sumac and salt in a spice mill and grind to a rough powder, or use a mortar and pestle.

Store in an airtight container in a cool dark place for up to several months — although the flavour is best if eaten within a few weeks of grinding.

EASY BEARNAISE SAUCE

Does just seeing the words 'double' and 'boiler' make you run the other way? It does me! If there's an easier way, I think we should do it. And this is the easier way. This is a brilliant and impressive sauce for serving on a piece of firepit grilled steak.

SERVES 4

3 large egg yolks

1 tablespoon tarragon vinegar

1 cup (250 g) unsalted butter

1 tablespoon finely chopped tarragon

2 spring onions (scallions), finely sliced

Put the egg yolks and vinegar in a food processor and pulse a few times.

Heat the butter in a small saucepan until bubbling hot and frothy. Be careful it doesn't burn.

While the butter is hot, with the motor running, start to pour it into the food processor in a steady stream until fully incorporated. Stir in the tarragon and spring onions while warm. Serve warm (it's tricky to reheat).

MUHUMARRA

There are many versions of this dip in Syria, although the combination of roasted red capsicums, walnuts and pomegranate molasses can be found in other parts of the Middle East, especially Turkey and Lebanon. Traditionally, this dip contains breadcrumbs. I have not included them here, so this version is coeliac friendly.

SERVES 6–8

3 large red capsicums (peppers)

3 tablespoons walnuts

1 teaspoon ground cumin

½ teaspoon cayenne pepper

2 tablespoons pomegranate molasses

2 tablespoons lemon juice

Your firepit is ready to cook on after about 2 hours of burning, when the timber is charcoal black, has transformed into red hot coals about the size of golf balls, and the smoke has all but subsided. To test for heat, you should not be able to hold the palm of your hand 5–10 cm (2–4 inches) above the grill for more than 2–3 seconds. Replace the grill over the firepit and give it around 10 minutes to heat up. (See page 9.)

Cook the capsicums on the firepit grill for 10–15 minutes, turning often, until the skins are blistered and blackened all over. Remove and leave to cool.

Peel and discard the skins. Cut the capsicums in half, scoop out and discard the seeds. Roughly chop the flesh and place in a food processor with the remaining ingredients.

Process to a smooth thick mixture and serve as a dip with flatbread or as a sauce with grilled meats. Keep in an airtight container in the fridge for up to 1 week.

REAL GARLIC BREAD

I say 'real' garlic bread because I am using real ingredients here. Let me explain. The few times that I went out to fine-dine as a kid in the 1970s, I remember garlic bread being served — and it was very special. Now it is often made with butter substitutes and garlic flakes. When made well, garlic bread is lovely. It is so easy to prepare ahead, ready to throw on the firepit and thrill your hungry guests.

SERVES 4

6 garlic cloves, finely chopped

1 teaspoon salt

3 tablespoons flat-leaf (Italian) parsley, finely chopped

½ cup (125 g) butter, at room temperature

1 sourdough baguette

Crush the garlic and salt together well. Mix with the parsley into the butter.

Your firepit is ready to cook on after about 2 hours of burning, when the timber is charcoal black, has transformed into red hot coals about the size of golf balls, and the smoke has all but subsided. To test for heat, you should not be able to hold the palm of your hand 5–10 cm (2–4 inches) above the grill for more than 2–3 seconds. Replace the grill over the firepit and give it around 10 minutes to heat up. (See page 9.)

Slice the baguette without cutting all the way through. Spread the garlic butter into the cuts. Wrap the bread in foil. Cook on the firepit grill for 8–10 minutes. Serve hot.

FIREPIT DAMPER

This bread epitomises Australian bush cooking. Like many good things, it originated out of necessity, created by stockmen on long journeys from the most basic of ingredients. There's a bit of an art to making damper — a bit like making scones — but, however it looks, it will always taste good!

2 cups (300 g) plain flour, plus extra, for dusting

1 teaspoon baking powder

1 teaspoon sea salt

½ cup (125 ml) milk

Mix the flour, baking powder and salt in a bowl and make a well in the centre.

In another bowl, mix the milk with the same amount of boiling water. Pour into the flour and mix quickly with a fork. Now use one hand to mix the dough: it will be a wet dough, so you might need to add a sprinkling of flour.

When the mixture no longer sticks to the side of the bowl, tip it out onto a lightly floured surface and knead for 1 minute until smooth. With lightly oiled hands, form the dough into a log about 10 cm (4 inches) wide and 15 cm (6 inches) long.

Lay a large sheet of foil on the work surface and place a sheet of baking paper on top. Lightly brush the baking paper with oil. Sit the dough at one long end of the baking paper. Loosely roll up the paper, then fold the ends to loosely enclose. Set aside for 30 minutes.

Your firepit is ready to cook on after about 2 hours of burning, when the timber is charcoal black, has transformed into red hot coals about the size of golf balls, and the smoke has all but subsided. To test for heat, you should not be able to hold the palm of your hand 5—10 cm (2—4 inches) above the grill for more than 2—3 seconds. Replace the grill over the firepit and give it around 10 minutes to heat up. (See page 9.)

Put a baking tray on the grill. Leave for 10 minutes or so to heat up.

Transfer the bread to the baking tray. Now move the tray to the edge of the firepit where the heat is less intense. Cook for 10 minutes. Turn the bread over and cook for a further 10—12 minutes, or until it makes a hollow sound when tapped. Leave wrapped for about 5 minutes, then transfer to a chopping board. Allow to cool for 10 minutes before serving.

TZATZIKI

This dip is best enjoyed as soon as it's made. It's great with vegie skewers or a piece of simple grilled chicken or fish. Or just serve as a dip with flatbread, while you wait for your firepit to heat up.

SERVES 8

1 Lebanese cucumber, grated

½ teaspoon sea salt

1½ cups (390 g) Greek yoghurt

2 garlic cloves, crushed

1 teaspoon ground cumin

Put the cucumber in a colander set over a bowl and sprinkle with the salt. Leave for 30 minutes for some of the liquid to drain off.

Mix the cucumber with the yoghurt, garlic and cumin.

INDEX

A

anchovies
  Anchovy butter 93
  Firepit chicken with green olive
    salsa verde 43
  Lamb chops with anchovy
    butter 93
  Veal cutlets with rosemary,
    anchovies and red wine 91
Anchovy butter 93
Arabian spice mix 194

B

Baked potatoes with herbed
  labneh 178
Barbecued snapper with
  Mexican salsa 124
basil
  Basil pesto 88
  Festive turkey 32
  Green curry chicken 46
  Lamb with basil pesto 88
Basil pesto 88
beef 9
  Beef rib-eye with horseradish
    butter 105
  Fragrant beef kefta 73
  Merguez sausages with harissa
    66
  Mixed meat grill 101
  New York cowboy 107
  Penang beef satay 78
  Roast beef fillet with paprika
    mayonnaise 94
  Rump steak with ginger, garlic
    and soy 98
  Spicy beef kebabs 83
  T-bones with café de Paris
    butter 69

see also veal
Beef rib-eye with horseradish
  butter 105
beer: Teriyaki and beer chicken
  36
bernaise sauce: Easy bearnaise
  sauce 195
Blackened bird 29
BLT, Chilli chicken 17
breads
  Cheat's garlic naan 22
  Firepit bread and tomato salad
    158
  Firepit damper 198
  Real garlic bread 197
Buccaneer chicken skewers 17
Butterflied lamb masala 104
butters
  Anchovy butter 93
  Café de Paris butter 69
  Horseradish butter 105
  Jalapeño butter 50
  Jalapeño, lime and parmesan
    butter 182, 194
  Lemon salsa butter 112
  Parmesan butter 165
  see also sauces

C

Café de Paris butter 69
Cajun spice rub 29
capsicum
  Chakchouka 169
  Muhumarra 196
  Piri piri marinade 40
  Piri piri spatchcock 40
  Swordfish kebabs 119
Chakchouka 169
Char siu glaze 97

Char siu lamb wraps 108
Chargrilled fennel with chilli and
  herbs 186
Charred tomato salsa with corn
  chips 173
Cheat's garlic naan 22
chicken 9
  Blackened bird 29
  Buccaneer chicken skewers
    17
  Chicken shawarma 54
  Chicken with jalapeño butter
    50
  Chilli chicken BLT 17
  Chilli yoghurt chicken 44
  Chimichurri chook 26
  Coconut tenderloins 58
  Creole chicken 63
  Fiery chicken chops 60
  Firepit chicken with green olive
    salsa verde 43
  Fragrant chicken parcels 17
  Green curry chicken 46
  Harissa chicken 45
  Honey hoisin chicken 14
  Keralan chicken 57
  Lebanese chicken with toum
    31
  Lemon chicken, feta and herb
    rolls 39
  Lemongrass and lime leaf
    chicken 25
  Piri piri spatchcock 40
  Quail with peanut and Thai
    herb pesto 30
  Sweet chilli and ginger chicken
    59
  Tandoori chicken with cheat's
    garlic naan 22

Teriyaki and beer chicken 36
Thai barbecued chicken 49
Chicken shawarma 54
Chicken with jalapeño butter 50
Chilli chicken BLT 17
Chilli yoghurt chicken 44
chillies
  Buccaneer chicken skewers
    17
  Chargrilled fennel with chilli
    and herbs 186
  Charred tomato salsa with corn
    chips 173
  Chicken with jalapeño butter
    50
  Chilli chicken BLT 17
  Chilli yoghurt chicken 44
  Fiery chicken chops 60
  Grilled corn with japapeño,
    lime and parmesan butter
    182, 194
  Hagen's pork neck 74
  Harissa 66
  Harissa chicken 45
  Jalapeño butter 50
  Jalapeño, lime and parmesan
    butter 182, 194
  Lime chilli sauce 17
  Lobster tails with chilli and
    garlic butter 131
  Merguez sausages with harissa
    66
  Nam jim (sweet chilli sauce)
    192
  New York cowboy 107
  Newspaper-wrapped salmon
    with fresh herbs, lemon and
    chilli 143
  Nuoc cham 80
  Quesadillas with pumpkin,
    pepitas and mozzarella 174
  Sicilian fish 132
  Sweet chilli and ginger chicken
    59
  Sweet chilli marinade 59
  Whole fish with jalapeño
    chillies, lemon and herbs 139

Chimichurri chook 26
Chinatown duck shanks 53
Chinatown pork 97
Chorizo skewers, Prawn and
  128
coconut
  Coconut tenderloins 58
  Green curry chicken 46
  Laksa prawn skewers 116
  Penang beef satay 78
  Seafood lemongrass skewers
    120
Coconut tenderloins 58
coriander
  Coriander and pepper rub
    49
  Hagen's pork neck 74
  Lemongrass, pepper and
    coriander pork skewers 80
  Nam jim (sweet chilli sauce)
    192
  Thai barbecued chicken 49
Coriander and pepper rub 49
corn
  Arabian spice mix 194
  Grilled corn with japapeño,
    lime and parmesan butter
    182, 194
  Spicy barbecued corn 166
corn chips: Charred tomato salsa
  with corn chips 173
Creole chicken 63
Creole sauce 63
cucumber: Tzatziki 199

D
damper, Firepit 198
dill
  Feta crème 157
  Whole baby trout with lemon
    and dill 115
  Whole fish with jalapeño
    chillies, lemon and herbs 139
dips 196, 199
dressings
  Bread and tomato salad
    dressing 158

Ginger and spring onion
  dressing 146
Spicy lemon dressing 177
Sweet and sour pumpkin
  dressing 185
Vegie salad dressing 150
duck shanks, Chinatown 53

E
Easy bearnaise sauce 195
eggplant
  Firepit barbie ghanoush 189
  Indian spiced eggplant 181
  Israeli eggplant salad 177
  Zucchini, eggplant and
    haloumi skewers 153

F
fennel
  Chargrilled fennel with chilli
    and herbs 186
  Sicilian fish 132
Festive turkey 32
feta
  Feta crème 157
  Lamb with feta, lemon and
    oregano 87
  Lemon chicken, feta and herb
    rolls 39
  Mushrooms with marinated
    feta 154
  Quesadillas with pumpkin,
    pepitas and mozzarella 174
  Saganaki prawns 127
  Spicy barbecued corn 166
  Sweet potatoes in jackets with
    feta crème 157
Fiery chicken chops 60
Firepit barbie ghanoush 189
Firepit bread and tomato salad
  158
Firepit chicken with green olive
  salsa verde 43
Firepit damper 198
firepit preparation 7–10
Firepit wedges 193
Firepit whiting 123

fish *see seafood*
Five-spice fish parcels 135
Five-spice sauce 135
Fragrant beef kefta 73
Fragrant chicken parcels 17
Fragrant five-spice vegetable
parcels 170
Fresh sambal 149

G
garlic
Cheat's garlic naan 22
Firepit barbie ghanoush
189
Lebanese chicken with toum
31
Lobster tails with chilli and
garlic butter 131
Nam jim (sweet chilli sauce)
192
Real garlic bread 197
Rump steak with ginger, garlic
and soy 98
ginger
Ginger and spring onion
dressing 146
Ocean trout fillet with ginger
and shallots 139
Rump steak with ginger, garlic
and soy 98
Sweet chilli and ginger chicken
59
Tofu and shiitake skewers with
ginger dressing 146
Whole snapper with ginger and
spring onions 136
Ginger and spring onion dressing
146
Green curry chicken 46
Green masala marinade 104
Green olive salsa 102
Green olive salsa verde 43
Grilled corn with japapeño, lime
and parmesan butter 182,
194
Grilled cos with parmesan butter
165

H
Hagen's pork neck 74
Haloumi skewers, Zucchini,
eggplant and 153
harissa
Harissa 66
Harissa chicken 45
Merguez sausages with harissa
66
Herbed labneh 178
herbs
Baked potatoes with herbed
labneh 178
Chargrilled fennel with chilli
and herbs 186
Firepit chicken with green olive
salsa verde 43
Green masala marinade 104
Green olive salsa 102
Green olive salsa verde 43
Herbed labneh 178
Lamb with green olive salsa
102
Lemon chicken, feta and herb
rolls 39
Newspaper-wrapped salmon
with fresh herbs, lemon and
chilli 143
Peanut and Thai herb pesto 30
Quail with peanut and Thai
herb pesto 30
Salsa verde 32
Whole fish with jalapeño
chillies, lemon and herbs 139
Honey hoisin chicken 14
horseradish
Beef rib-eye with horseradish
butter 105
Horseradish butter 105

I
Indian cottage cheese: Paneer
skewers with tomato relish
162
Indian spiced eggplant 181
involtini, Veal and provolone 78
Israeli eggplant salad 177

J
Jalapeño butter 50
Jalapeño, lime and parmesan
butter 182, 194

K
kebabs
Lamb kebabs with spiced
yoghurt 70
Smoky pork kebabs 84
Spicy beef kebabs 83
Swordfish kebabs 119
Keralan chicken 57

L
labneh
Baked potatoes with herbed
labneh 178
Herbed labneh 178
Indian spiced eggplant 181
Laksa prawn skewers 116
lamb 9
Butterflied lamb masala 104
Char siu lamb wraps 108
Lamb chops with anchovy
butter 93
Lamb kebabs with spiced
yoghurt 70
Lamb with basil pesto 88
Lamb with feta, lemon and
oregano 87
Lamb with green olive salsa
102
Merguez sausages with harissa
66
Mixed meat grill 101
Sheftalia 92
Lamb chops with anchovy butter
93
Lamb kebabs with spiced
yoghurt 70
Lamb with basil pesto 88
Lamb with feta, lemon and
oregano 87
Lamb with green olive salsa
102
Lebanese chicken with toum 31

Lemon chicken, feta and herb
    rolls 39
Lemon salsa butter 112
lemongrass
  Lemongrass and lime leaf
      chicken 25
  Lemongrass, pepper and
      coriander pork skewers 80
  Lime leaf and lemongrass tofu
      161
  Seafood lemongrass skewers
      120
Lemongrass and lime leaf
    chicken 25
Lemongrass, pepper and
    coriander pork skewers 80
lemons
  Firepit barbie ghanoush 189
  Keralan chicken 57
  Lamb with feta, lemon and
      oregano 87
  Lemon salsa butter 112
  Muhumarra 196
  Newspaper-wrapped salmon
      with fresh herbs, lemon and
      chilli 143
  Parchment baked whiting with
      lemon salsa sauce 112
  Sicilian fish 132
  Spicy lemon dressing 177
  Whole baby trout with lemon
      and dill 115
  Whole fish with jalapeño
      chillies, lemon and herbs 139
lettuce
  Chilli chicken BLT 17
  Grilled cos with parmesan
      butter 165
Lime and pepper sauce 35
Lime and turmeric tofu steaks
    with fresh sambal 149
Lime chilli sauce 17
Lime leaf and lemongrass tofu
    161
limes
  Buccaneer chicken skewers
      17

Grilled corn with japapeño,
    lime and parmesan butter
    182, 194
Jalapeño, lime and parmesan
    butter 182, 194
Laksa prawn skewers 116
Lemongrass and lime leaf
    chicken 25
Lime and pepper sauce 35
Lime and turmeric tofu steaks
    with fresh sambal 149
Lime chilli sauce 17
Lime leaf and lemongrass tofu
    161
Spiced quail with Vietnamese
    lime and pepper dipping
    sauce 35
Lobster tails with chilli and garlic
    butter 131

M
marinades 40, 59, 78, 104
mayonnaise
  Paprika mayonnaise 94
  Roast beef fillet with paprika
      mayonnaise 94
meatballs
  Fragrant beef kefta 73
  Sheftalia 92
Merguez sausages with harissa
    66
Mexican salsa 124
Mixed meat grill 101
mozzarella, Quesadillas with
    pumpkin, pepitas and 174
Muhumarra 196
mushrooms
  Mushrooms with marinated
      feta 154
  Tofu and shiitake skewers with
      ginger dressing 146
Mushrooms with marinated feta
    154

N
naan, Cheat's garlic 22
Nam jim (sweet chilli sauce) 192

New York cowboy 107
New York cowboy spice rub 107
Newspaper-wrapped salmon
    with fresh herbs, lemon and
    chilli 143
Nuoc cham 80

O
Ocean trout fillet with ginger and
    shallots 139
olives
  Firepit chicken with green olive
      salsa verde 43
  Green olive salsa 102
  Green olive salsa verde 43
  Lamb with green olive salsa
      102
oregano, Lamb with feta, lemon
    and 87

P
Paneer skewers with tomato
    relish 162
paprika
  New York cowboy 107
  Paprika mayonnaise 94
  Roast beef fillet with paprika
      mayonnaise 94
  Smoky pork kebabs 84
Paprika mayonnaise 94
Parchment baked whiting with
    lemon salsa sauce 112
parmesan
  Grilled corn with japapeño,
      lime and parmesan butter
      182
  Grilled cos with parmesan
      butter 165
  Jalapeño, lime and parmesan
      butter 182, 194
  Parmesan butter 165
Parmesan butter 165
Peanut and Thai herb pesto 30
peanuts
  Peanut and Thai herb pesto 30
  Penang beef satay 78
  Penang satay marinade 78

Quail with peanut and Thai herb pesto 30
Penang beef satay 78
Penang satay marinade 78
pepitas, Quesadillas with pumpkin, mozzarella and 174
pepper
    Coriander and pepper rub 49
    Lemongrass, pepper and coriander pork skewers 80
    Lime and pepper sauce 35
    Spiced quail with Vietnamese lime and pepper dipping sauce 35
    Thai barbecued chicken 49
pesto 30, 88
Piri piri spatchcock 40
pork 9
    Chinatown pork 97
    Hagen's pork neck 74
    Lemongrass, pepper and coriander pork skewers 80
    Pork carnitas 77
    Smoky pork kebabs 84
Pork carnitas 77
potatoes
    Baked potatoes with herbed labneh 178
    Firepit wedges 193
Prawn and chorizo skewers 128
prawns
    Prawn and chorizo skewers 128
    Saganaki prawns 127
    Seafood lemongrass skewers 120
provolone cheese: Veal and provolone involtini 78
pumpkin
    Quesadillas with pumpkin, pepitas and mozzarella 174
    Sweet and sour pumpkin 185

Q
quail
    Quail with peanut and Thai herb pesto 30
    Spiced quail with Vietnamese lime and pepper dipping sauce 35
    Quesadillas with pumpkin, pepitas and mozzarella 174

R
Real garlic bread 197
Roast beef fillet with paprika mayonnaise 94
rosemary, Veal cutlets with anchovies and red wine 91
Rump steak with ginger, garlic and soy 98

S
Saganaki prawns 127
salads
    Firepit bread and tomato salad 158
    Israeli eggplant salad 177
    Ultimate firepit vegie salad 150
Salsa verde 32
Sambal, fresh 149
Satay, Penang beef 78
sauces
    Charred tomato salsa with corn chips 173
    Easy bearnaise sauce 195
    Five-spice sauce 135
    Green olive salsa 102
    Green salsa verde 43
    Lemon salsa butter 112
    Mexican salsa 124
    Nam jim (sweet chilli sauce) 192
    Salsa verde 32
    see also butters
seafood 10
    Barbecued snapper with Mexican salsa 124
    Firepit whiting 123
    Five-spice fish parcels 135
    Laksa prawn skewers 116
    Lobster tails with chilli and garlic butter 131
    Newspaper-wrapped salmon with fresh herbs, lemon and chilli 143
    Ocean trout fillet with ginger and shallots 139
    Parchment baked whiting with lemon salsa sauce 112
    Prawn and chorizo skewers 128
    Saganaki prawns 127
    Seafood lemongrass skewers 120
    Sicilian fish 132
    Swordfish kebabs 119
    Whole baby trout with lemon and dill 115
    Whole fish with jalapeño chillies, lemon and herbs 139
    Whole snapper with ginger and spring onions 136
Seafood lemongrass skewers 120
shallots
    Charred tomato salsa with corn chips 173
    Ocean trout fillet with ginger and shallots 139
Shawarma, Chicken 54
Sheftalia 92
Sicilian fish 132
Smoky pork kebabs 84
soy sauce
    Fragrant chicken parcels 17
    Rump steak with ginger, garlic and soy 98
    Teriyaki and beer chicken 36
Spatchcock, Piri piri 40
Spiced quail with Vietnamese lime and pepper dipping sauce 35
Spicy barbecued corn 166
Spicy beef kebabs 83
Spicy lemon dressing 177

spring onions
Ginger and spring onion
dressing 146
Whole snapper with ginger and
spring onions 136
Sweet and sour pumpkin 185
Sweet chilli and ginger chicken
59
Sweet chilli marinade 59
Sweet potatoes in jackets with
feta crème 157
Swordfish kebabs 119

T
T-bones with café de Paris
butter 69
Tandoori chicken with cheat's
garlic naan 22
Teriyaki and beer chicken
36
Thai barbecued chicken 49
tofu
Lime and turmeric tofu steaks
with fresh sambal 149
Lime leaf and lemongrass tofu
161
Tofu and shiitake skewers with
ginger dressing 146
Tomato relish 162
tomatoes
Chakchouka 169
Charred tomato salsa with corn
chips 173
Chilli chicken BLT 17
Firepit bread and tomato salad
158
Israeli eggplant salad 177
Saganaki prawns 127
Swordfish kebabs 119
Tofu and shiitake skewers with
ginger dressing 146
Tomato relish 162
Toum, Lebanese chicken with
31
trout
Ocean trout fillet with ginger
and shallots 139

Whole baby trout with lemon
and dill 115
Turkey, Festive 32
Turmeric, Lime and turmeric tofu
steaks with fresh sambal 149
Tzatziki 199

U
Ultimate firepit vegie salad 150

V
Veal and provolone involtini 78
Veal cutlets with rosemary,
anchovies and red wine 91
vegetables 10
Baked potatoes with herbed
labneh 178
Chakchouka 169
Chargrilled fennel with chilli
and herbs 186
Charred tomato salsa with corn
chips 173
Firepit barbie ghanoush 189
Firepit bread and tomato salad
158
Firepit wedges 193
Fragrant five-spice vegetable
parcels 170
Grilled corn with japapeño,
lime and parmesan butter
182, 194
Grilled cos with parmesan
butter 165
Indian spiced eggplant 181
Israeli eggplant salad 177
Lime and turmeric tofu steaks
with fresh sambal 149
Lime leaf and lemongrass tofu
161
Muhumarra 196
Mushrooms with marinated
feta 154
Paneer skewers with tomato
relish 162
Quesadillas with pumpkin,
pepitas and mozzarella 174
Spicy barbecued corn 166

Sweet and sour pumpkin 185
Sweet potatoes in jackets with
feta crème 157
Tofu and shiitake skewers with
ginger dressing 146
Ultimate firepit vegie salad
150
Zucchini, eggplant and
haloumi skewers 153

W
Whole baby trout with lemon and
dill 115
Whole fish with jalapeño chillies,
lemon and herbs 139
Whole snapper with ginger and
spring onions 136
wraps, Char siu lamb 108

Y
yoghurt
Chilli yoghurt chicken 44
Lamb kebabs with spiced
yoghurt 70
Tandoori chicken with cheat's
garlic naan 22
Tzatziki 199

Z
Zucchini, eggplant and haloumi
skewers 153

This edition published in 2021 by Murdoch Books, an imprint of Allen & Unwin

Murdoch Books Australia
83 Alexander Street
Crows Nest NSW 2065
Phone: +61 (0)2 8425 0100
murdochbooks.com.au
info@murdochbooks.com.au

Murdoch Books UK
Erico House, 6th Floor
93–99 Upper Richmond Road
Putney, London SW15 2TG
Phone: +44 (0) 20 8785 5995
www.murdochbooks.co.uk
info@murdochbooks.co.uk

For corporate orders and custom publishing, contact our business development team
at salesenquiries@murdochbooks.com.au

Publisher: Corinne Roberts
Editorial manager: Jane Price
Design manager: Vivien Valk
Designer: Susanne Geppert
Design concept: Trisha Garner
Photography: Alan Benson, Nicky Ryan and Brett Stevens
Stylists: Jane Hann, Lynsey Fryers, Sarah O'Brien and Matt Page
Food preparation for photography: Jimmy Callaway
Production Director: Lou Playfair

ISBN 9 781 92235 190 6 Australia
ISBN 9 781 92261 602 9 UK

A catalogue record for this book is available from the National Library of Australia

A catalogue record for this book is available from the British Library

Colour reproduction by Splitting Image Colour Studio Pty Ltd, Clayton, Victoria
Printed by C&C Offset Printing Co. Ltd., China